Religious Gende

Xavier Boote

Abstract

This dissertation includes three essays that present a quantitative analysis of the policy implications of gender equality and religious attitudes as predictors of terrorism at the state level using a broad dataset. Essay one focuses on impact of gender equality, especially women's political empowerment on terrorism, both domestic and transnational. The second essay examines both gender equality attitudes and actual outcomes in social, economic and political spheres, to measure their effect on terrorism. The third essay analyzes the relation of religiousness in a society with incidents and lethality of terrorism. The overall findings of this thesis suggest that attitudes and norms of gender equality matter with regard to terrorism, but practices and outcomes matter more. Results also indicate that religious attitudes of a society are associated with lethality of terror attack. These findings have important policy implications for rethinking prevention of terrorism in an effective and innovative manner. The results strongly support investment in women's rights programs, promotion of religious tolerance and provision of social services as indirect policy solutions to curb the conditions that foster terrorism.

TABLE OF CONTENTS

Abstract iii

Acknowledgements v

Chapter 1: Background and Introduction to three essays 1

    1.1   Introduction 1

    1.2   Definition and Concept of Terrorism 5

    1.3   Essays 13

    1.4   Strengths and Limitations 16

Chapter 2: Why her voice matters: The impact of Women's Rights on how States experience Terrorism 22

    2.1   Introduction 22

    2.2   Literature Review 26

        2.2.1 Gender and Terrorism 28

        2.2.2 Terrorism and Economic Development 33

        2.2.3 Terrorism and Political Environment 34

        2.2.4 Domestic and Transnational Terrorism 37

    2.3   Research Design 38

    2.4   Estimation 46

    2.5   Interpretation 48

    2.6   Conclusion 52

Chapter 3: Actions speak louder than words: Measuring the Impact of Gender Equality Attitudes and Outcomes as Deterrents of Terrorism 70

    3.1   Introduction 70

3.2 Literature Review 72

    3.2.1 Terrorism and Culture 74

    3.2.2 Connection between Gender Equality and Terrorism 76

3.3 Research Design 83

3.4 Estimation 89

3.5 Interpretation 90

3.6 Conclusion 94

Chapter 4: Killing in the name of God: Religion and Lethality of Terrorist Attacks 113

    4.1 Introduction 113

    4.2 Links between Religion and Terrorism 119

        4.2.1 Use of 'othering' in Religious Terrorism 121

        4.2.2. Mutual Aid and Lethality 127

        4.2.3 Suicide Terrorism and Lethality 129

        4.2.4 Islamic Fundamentalism and Lethality 131

        4.2.5 Rise in Religious Terrorism 132

    4.3 Research Design 135

    4.4 Estimation 139

    4.5 Interpretation 142

    4.6 Conclusion 144

Chapter 1: Background and Introduction to three essays

1.1 Introduction

Since September 11, 2001, the issue of terrorism has gained tremendous attention in the media, political arena, and academic scholarship. In spite of the growing body of terrorism research, the relation of gender equality and religion to terrorism is still under-researched especially in empirical work. This study presents a quantitative analysis of the policy implications of gender equality and religious attitudes as predictors of terrorism at the state level. The overall findings of this thesis suggest that attitudes and norms of gender equality matter with regard to terrorism, but practices and outcomes matter more. Results also indicate that religious attitudes of a society are associated with lethality of a terror attack[1].

Terrorism is a political phenomenon with social roots and is influenced by the cultural, socio-economic and political environment (Crenshaw, 1981, 2010; McCormick, 2003; Newman, 2006; Robison, 2010). Previous research examines state level factors like democracy, economic factors, population growth and size, youth bulge, government spending on social welfare policies, political and financial decentralization, geography and temporal proximity to terrorism as predictors of terrorism (Abadie, 2006; Burgoon, 2006; Dreher & Fischer, 2011; Enders & Sandler, 2002; Eubank & Weinberg, 1994, 2001; Krieger & Meierrieks, 2010; Li, 2005; Li & Schaub, 2004; Midlarsky, Crenshaw,

---

[1] By lethality I mean the number of people killed in a terror attack.

& Yoshida, 1980; Urdal, 2006). Although there are links between terrorism and the environment that produces it, no set of analysis can provide a complete deterministic explanation of the conditions that produce terrorism. So far limited attention has been paid to state level indicators of gender equality and religious attitudes, yet both are significant aspects of the environment that influences terrorism. This study fills an important research gap by empirically testing the relation of gender inequality and religion with terrorism.

The overarching premise driving this analysis is to study potential causes and consequences of terrorism using a broad dataset. Not all countries experience the same amount of terrorism. This leads to the question: Why would terrorists attack certain countries and not others? The fundamental purpose of this thesis is to quantify conditions, both attitudes and practices, which make countries an attractive target for terrorist attacks. Adopting gender as an analytical variable and measuring state-level of terrorism, this dissertation uses a feminist perspective to deconstruct androcentric assumptions that terrorism is gender neutral. This thesis propels a discussion to revise and revisit the dominant terrorism research paradigms. Looking at religious attitudes as predictors of lethality of an attack provides unique insights about the relationship of religion and terrorism.

This dissertation argues that both gender equality and religiousness are strong indicators of the socio-cultural environment and conditions that produce terrorism. The way societies treat women has an impact on how much terrorism they experience. Also the religious attitudes of a society impact the severity of an attack. Gender equality and religiousness are good predictors of the level and lethality of terrorism experienced by a state. Actual outcomes[2] of gender equality, rather than cultural norms, are stronger predictors of terrorism. They are negatively related to terrorism i.e. increasing gender equality outcomes significantly reduces terrorism, which makes them suitable for counterterrorism measures and policies. Furthermore, more religious societies are more vulnerable to lethal terrorism. More religiosity indicates a society that is less tolerant of religious diversity and freedom, and it suggests that violent religious terrorists find more support in religious societies than less religious ones.

The scope of this dissertation is an empirical examination of state level norms and practices of gender equality and religiousness as they relate to terrorism in a country. Scholars agree that terrorism is a highly complex and diverse phenomenon and there is no 'one size fits all' explanation for the causes and organizational dynamics behind this phenomenon. Therefore terrorism has to be engaged with an inter-disciplinary approach and analyzed at different levels i.e. micro, meso and macro, to construct a deeper understanding of its nature and patterns. At the micro level, the individual psychology and case studies are indeed important in understanding terrorism, but are insufficient to fully comprehend the global patterns of terrorism. At the meso level, there is growing literature studying terrorist group dynamics, organizational psychology and social networks, which provides powerful analytic tools to capture the various layers of complexity. However the macro level broadens the unit of analysis, and focuses at the state level factors that generate or deter terrorism. Given the long history and patterns of terrorism over time, both domestic and transnational, there is tremendous research

---

[2] By outcomes I mean the actual progress made towards women's empowerment measured by female literacy, female labor participation and women's representation in the parliament. I provide a working definition of 'outcomes' in my second essay.

potential in analyzing the driving factors of terrorism at the macro level, which provides a more comprehensive understanding of the complex nature and patterns of global terrorism. State level analysis offers room to study patterns, causes, factors, and driving forces behind terrorism in a broader fashion that might not be captured at the individual or organizational level. Most of the data in this dissertation is drawn from Global Terrorism Database (LaFree & Dugan, 2007), World values Survey ("World Values Survey ", 2000) and the Quality of Government (Teorell, 2011).

This thesis includes three essays that investigate the relationship of gender equality and religion with terrorism in a country from a public policy perspective. Essay one focuses on gender equality indicators, especially women's political empowerment, as predictor of terrorism. The second essay tests for both gender equality attitudes and actual outcomes in social, economic and political spheres, to measure their impact on terrorism. In these two studies making a cross-national time series quantitative analysis of gender equality attitudes and women rights as predictors of terrorism provides empirical evidence as to how gender inequality and terrorism are strongly associated. The third essay analyzes the relation of religiousness in a society with incidents and lethality of terrorism. The empirical analysis of impact of religious attitudes on terrorism provides innovative insights about the role of religion in violent terrorism.

The following section presents a brief discussion of the definition and concept of terrorism, including domestic and transnational terrorism, to provide a broad understanding of the meaning of the term terrorism. It also presents a brief outline of how gender equality and religion are related to terrorism. This research draws motivation and ideas from previous literature on predictors of terrorism. More detailed review of the relevant past literature is presented in each of three essays.

1.2 Definition and Concept of Terrorism

Although terrorism has long been debated, there is little consensus in the literature over its definition. As early as 1988, Schmid and Jongman (1988) found over 100 definitions of terrorism. The definition even varies over the different departments in the US government, depending on their approach and understanding of terrorism. However scholars do agree that it is a highly subjective term with negative connotations, generally applied to individuals and groups one disagrees with, because it imposes a moral judgment on them (Crenshaw, 1989; Hoffman, 1999; Jenkins, 1980). Over the years it has evolved into a pejorative term such that even terrorist organizations choose not to label themselves as terrorists and prefer neutral terms like freedom fighters, social revolutionaries or liberation movements (Hoffman, 2006). Definitional debate persists over whether the term should be defined based on the act (Jenkins, 1980; Todd Sandler, 2003)[3], actor (Hoffman, 1999), or the target and audience of violence (Krueger, 2008; Schmid & Jongman, 1988).

Labeling a group or person as terrorist has significant consequences for them. Governments gain moral superiority and power over their enemies when they define them as terrorists and it justifies use of force and military action to eliminate them (Jenkins, 1980; White, 2012). There is little consensus in the literature whether states can be

---

[3] Sandler (2003) defines terrorism as "the premeditated use, or threat of use, of extra-normal violence or brutality to gain a political objective through intimidation or fear of a targeted audience" (p780)

terrorists[4]. In this regard Hoffman (2006) argues that governments are essentially 'good' because they operate within the domain of regulations and terrorists are 'evil' because they operate outside the legitimate realm of law. On the other hand Crenshaw (1981) asserts, 'terrorism occurs both in the context of violent resistance to the state as well in the service of the state interest' (p379). According to Kydd and Walter (2006) terrorism is the use of violence against civilians by non-state actors to achieve political goals. While transnational terrorism more often targets civilians, but domestic terrorism is often aimed at combatants, state law enforcement and military personnel in a systematic manner (Sánchez-Cuenca & de la Calle, 2009).

The brief overview of the literature demonstrates that definition of terrorism is awkwardly fluid and subjective. Explaining the fluid and nebulous nature of terrorism, Schmid (1992) states that this term is actually a social construct and its meaning changes depending on the social reality of the group defining it. Nevertheless by and large, most of the definitions of terrorism agree that it is a violent, political act against non-combatants/ civilians or combatants, to intimidate and influence a wider target audience.

Definition in this study is prescribed by the dataset. This study employs the definitional criteria of Global Terrorism Dataset (LaFree & Dugan, 2007) to define terrorism. GTD criteria for recording an event as a terrorist event includes that the event has to be intentional, be violent or entail threat of it, carried out by non-state actors outside the realm of legitimate warfare. Also one of the two conditions must be fulfilled

---

[4] There is inconclusive debate that whether state or non-state actors are terrorists. In his definition of terrorism, Jenkins (1980) focuses on the act rather than actor, which suggests that even state actors can be regarded as terrorists if they employ terrorist tactics. On the other hand Hoffman (1999) believes terrorism needs to be defined by the identity of the actor and not by the nature of the act. According to him only non-state actors are defined as terrorists.

that the attack is carried out to influence a group larger than the immediate target and/ or the attack has a political, social, religious or ideological goal. This data is the most comprehensive publically available dataset on terrorism, including both domestic and transnational attacks. However this data has some limitation i.e. it is based on media reports and bias might be introduced due to under-reporting, also it does not make a distinction between domestic and transnational terrorism. GTD records the location of the terrorist attack but has no information about the nationality of the perpetuator. The perpetuator can be citizen of the state or a foreign national. This distinction is important for research of country level conditions that produce terrorism and the factors that make a country an attractive target. This thesis employs the dataset developed by Enders, Sandler, and Gaibulloev (2011), which separates domestic and transnational terrorist attacks in GTD[5].

Domestic and Transnational Terrorism:

A terror attack is referred to as domestic terrorism when the victim, perpetuator and audience all belong to the same country, while transnational terrorism involves more than one country (Enders & Sandler, 2002; Enders et al., 2011). Even though transnational terrorism stirs up more media attention, domestic terrorism occurs three to four times more often than transnational terrorist events in GTD (Enders et al., 2011).

---

[5] There are 82,536 terrorist incidents in GTD for 1970–2007, after applying three criteria: 'the attack is perpetrated for a political, socio- economic, or religious motive; the attack is intended to coerce, intimidate, or send a message to a wider audience than the immediate victim(s); and the attack is beyond the boundaries set by international humanitarian law' p322 (Enders et al., 2011). The authors are left with 66,383 terrorist incidents to classify as domestic or transnational. Based on a five-step procedure, they list 12,862 transnational terrorist incidents; this number is similar to ITERATE which contains 12,784 transnational terrorist incidents for the same time interval. Whenever there is missing or unknown information the event is classified as unknown. So they determined 7,108 incidents as uncertain and identified 46,413 incidents as domestic incidents.

Domestic terrorism is also more violent than transnational terrorism (Sánchez-Cuenca & de la Calle, 2009). Most of the 98,000 terrorist incidents/attacks recorded in GTD are of domestic nature, compared to the 12,000 number of attacks recorded in the International Terrorism: Attributes of Terrorist Events dataset, which contains information on only transnational attacks from 1968-2004. The MIPT Terrorism Knowledge Base dataset recorded 26,445 fatalities during 1998- 2005, out of which only 6447 were result of transnational terrorism including 3000 fatalities from the September 11, 2001 attacks (Asal & Rethemeyer, 2008b).

Domestic and transnational terrorism are distinguished by the nationality of the actors involved in the attack, yet both display such similar patterns and consequences that some scholars believe this distinction is irrelevant (Sánchez-Cuenca & de la Calle, 2009). Recent research shows that both domestic and transnational terrorism are driven by same factors (Kis-Katos, Liebert, & Schulze, 2011).

Nevertheless according to Enders et al. (2011) there are reasons to believe that there is correlation between domestic and transnational terrorism. Domestic terrorism may result in collateral damage to international interests, giving rise to transnational terrorism. Domestic terrorists may include transnational terrorism as a strategy to gain more media attention. They might even seek refuge in neighboring countries, creating a contagion effect where there is more probability for a country to experience terrorism if its neighboring country does (Midlarsky et al., 1980). Because of social networks in terrorists organizations, Asal and Rethemeyer (2006) find there is evidence of a 'copy-cat' effect of learning from each other's tactics and innovation. In order to carry out a successful transnational attack, terrorist organizations need local/ domestic support from terrorist groups or extremist accomplices in the target country (Belli, 2012).

Other reasons for linkages between domestic and transnational terrorism include operating costs and political environment. Terrorists seek softer targets and lower operating cost, so they may calculate greater target opportunities outside their base country. Such determinants raise (or lower) the operating cost, causing decline (or increase) in terrorist activity (Lai, 2007a). Political events and foreign policy decisions generate backlash which might result in both domestic and transnational terrorism. Many terrorist organizations engage in both domestic and transnational terrorism, depending on their ideology, goal and audience. Also research shows that a country experiencing domestic terrorism is more likely to be target of transnational terrorism. With regard to increasing operating cost of terrorist group attention must be paid to domestic terrorism along with transnational terrorism, as both pose a threat to the global community. Most of the studies on determinants of terrorism focus on transnational terrorism (Enders & Sandler, 2000, 2002; Li, 2005; Li & Schaub, 2004; Piazza, 2008a; Robison, 2010). One of the reasons could be that data on domestic attacks like GTD has only recently become available.

Looking at unconventional but significant measures of terrorism, this study analyzes the connections of gender equality and religiousness with both domestic and transitional terrorism.

Gender equality and Terrorism:

Gender matters in the theory and practice of security studies. It is an important and often overlooked factor needed to understand international security, conceptually. It is important in analyzing causes and predicting outcomes, thinking for solutions and promoting positive change (Sjoberg, 2010; Tickner, 1992). Until recently the role of women's empowerment has not been extensively examined in an empirical fashion for conflict in general (Caprioli, 2005) or as it relates to levels of terrorism (Robison, 2010).

There is evidence that increased gender equality in the society, judged by women's participation in economic, social and political spheres would result in less and fewer militarized disputes at an international level (Melander, 2005). Research shows that a positive relationship exists between gender equality in a state and its peaceful relations with other states (Caprioli, 2000, 2003a, 2003b; Caprioli & Boyer, 2001; Regan & Paskeviciute, 2003). Gender inequality leads to more intrastate conflict and greater gender equality contributes to peace within states (Caprioli, 2005). In fact state violence may in turn lead to higher levels of gender violence. The physical, political, social and economic violence against women is a significant indicator of other forms of state violence (Caiazza, 2001; Hudson, 2012; Hudson, Caprioli, Ballif-Spanvill, McDermott, & Emmett, 2008)

The research on women and terrorism done so far is mostly qualitative (Alison, 2004; Berko & Erez, 2007; Bloom, 2005, 2011; Cook, 2005; Cunningham, 2003; Friedman, 2008; Galvin, 1983; Gentry, 2009; Gunawardena, 2006; Kunz & Sjoberg, 2009; Nacos, 2005; Ness, 2005; O'Rourke, 2009; Schweitzer, 2006; Speckhard, 2008; Stack, 2011; Von Knop, 2007; Weinberg & Eubank, 2011) and limited attention has been paid to testing the relationship of gender and terrorism in a quantitative manner. A major reason for this could be the lack of reliable data. Most of the qualitative studies focus on factors motivating women to become terrorists, and few studies have examined gender equality at the country level as a predictor of terrorism (Robison, 2010).

This study assumes that women's political empowerment has a stronger impact on the level of terrorism in a country. I hypothesize that while women's economic and political inclusion has an impact, women attaining positions of political power is a stronger predictor of terrorism because then women can actually impact policy. The first essay tests this assumption. Using World Values Survey data, the second essay extends the analysis to explore if and how cultural attitudes and actual outcomes of gender equality in a society impacts terrorism.

Religion and Terrorism:

The links between violence and religion are age old and not limited to one religious tradition. This does not mean that religion is violent per se but according to Huber (2011) it plays a critical role in aggravating violence by sanctifying acts of violence. This relationship between religion and violence is not limited to any specific region, country, denomination, group or class, but it is endemic and global (Fox, 2004; Fox & Sandler, 2004; Hoffman, 1995, 2006; Juergensmeyer, 2001, 2003; Ranstorp, 1996). The sharp increase in contemporary religious terrorism has made it a major concern both for policy makers and academics. Religious terrorism becomes more dangerous and vicious because it evokes religion to justify acts of violence and killing in the name of a holy entity. Religion provides a popular motivation for violence and terrorism, with sacred texts or clerical authority sanctifying acts of terror (Atran & Ginges, 2012; Juergensmeyer, 2003). Juergensmeyer (2003) explains that religious justifications are rooted in the practice of 'othering' a population, and this requires a clear divide between members and non-members based on religion or ethnicity. During conflict, religion often provides identity markers for in-group and out-group members. Hence othering an enemy makes their indiscriminate killing easier and justified.

The other factors that affect religious terrorism and make it more lethal are its ideology and capability. Analyzing why certain terrorist organizations kill more than others, Asal and Rethemeyer (2008b) find empirical evidence that organizations which invoke a super natural audience through religious ideologies are more lethal. Terrorist groups, although clandestine organizations, are dependent on social networks and community support in order to carry out their operations and attacks. To gain public support in religious societies religious extremists operate provide essential services to the poor and marginalized communities through mutual aid (Berman, 2009; Iannaccone & Berman, 2006). The social services provided to these populations gain them important community support and essential human capital, making it easier to pitch the in-group against the out-group, marked as 'other'. In fact widespread discontent and dissatisfaction provides a sympathetic support pool to extremists (Oberschall, 2004). Research also shows that exclusion of ethnic minority groups from government coalition is linked to terrorism, as extremist factions within minority groups use religion as a mobilizing force to perpetuate terrorism (Satana, Inman, & Birnir, 2013).

Given the links between religion and terrorism, it is surprising that there is so little quantitative research examining the impact of religious attitudes on terrorism at the country level. The World Values Survey data provides an opportunity to test the effect of religious attitudes on terrorism on a large number of countries, over a relatively longer period of time.

1.3 Essays

To investigate the effects of gender equality and religiousness on terrorism this thesis presents three essays.

Essay one: Why her voice matters: Impact of Women's Rights on how States experience Terrorism

This study engages in a gendered analysis of terrorism. Controlling for various predictors of terrorism, it examines the impact of gender equality on how much terrorism a country experiences. It is a cross-national time series quantitative analysis of women's rights as predictors of terrorism, using data from the Global Terrorism Database (GTD) for 155 countries from 1981-2002. The results suggest that women's political empowerment has a negative and significant relationship with terrorism, both domestic and transnational. These results mean that a higher number of women in parliament is strongly associated with fewer terrorist attacks in a country in a particular year.

This is an innovative study as it examines impact of domestic gender equality on domestic and translational terrorism separately. Previous studies have only examined impact of women's rights on transnational terrorism (Robison, 2010). The analysis is further extended to examine the effect of gender equality by regime type and level of economic development of a country. The findings show that women's political rights are a stronger deterrent to terrorism in democracies and countries with higher economic development. The study offers important policy implications for long-term counter terrorism strategies. It suggests that more women in higher decision-making bodies are able to use their collective agency to build peaceful societies, which has a dampening effect on terrorism. Higher gender equality in a society may reflect an inclusive and just society that provides democratic avenues to its population to address the grievances and frustrations that propel terrorism.

Essay two: Actions speak louder than words: Measuring the impact of Gender Equality attitudes and outcomes as deterrents of Terrorism

This essay looks at the cultural attitudes and actual outcomes of gender equality to measure their impact on terrorism. It includes cross-national times series analysis for 57 countries for the period 1994-2002 using World Values Survey and Global Terrorism Database. The results suggest that women's actual advancement and equality in higher education, jobs and political representation are more effective in reducing terrorism, than cultural attitudes supporting these rights. The results show that even for domestic and transnational terrorism, actual progress made in women's empowerment in social, economic and political spheres has a significant and consistently negative impact on terrorism. These findings have important policy implications for counter terrorism measures to focus more on actual outcomes of gender equality rather than public opinion and attitudes. It also draws attention to the gap between perceived notions and actual results. This gap has broader and significant policy implications for issues and debates of social justice for marginalized communities. The public opinion and perception of inequality might be different from the actual reality, so more attention should be focused on better data collection and understanding of actual outcomes of efforts for equality and social justice for disadvantaged groups and communities.

Essay three: Killing in the name of God: Religion and Lethality of Terrorist Attacks

The third essay is an analysis of impact of religious attitudes on the lethality of a terrorist attack, examining 76 countries over the period 1981 to 2004 using Global Terrorism Database (GTD) and World Values Survey (WVS). The results of this cross-national time series study show that more religious societies experience more lethal terrorism. It is observed that Islamic fundamentalism is often associated with terrorism. I test the impact of percentage of Muslim population in a society on terrorism. The results show no statistically significant relationship between Muslim population and number of people killed in an attack.

The results posit a causal relationship between religion and terrorism, based on the practices of 'othering' and mutual aid. Religion is one way to mark people as in-group and out-group during conflict and political unrest. Religious extremists find it easier to win sympathizers and gain community support in religious societies than less religious ones. This makes it easier to justify killing people defined as out-group or other. In addition, religious organizations provide social services through mutual aid where state fails to provide them and can exploit social service gaps for deadly purposes. The findings in this essay suggest that more religious societies are perhaps less tolerant of religious diversity and freedom, and often use religion as a mobilizing force to perpetuate terrorism. Based on these findings I suggest long term policy solutions to terrorism, especially religiously motivated terrorism, for promoting religious tolerance and equality, to build stronger social welfare systems to support marginalized communities and create safe, just and inclusive society.

1.4 Strengths and Limitations

This study contributes to the scholarship on understanding the explanatory factors for terrorism. It presents an innovative empirical analysis of terrorism and focuses on unconventional explanatory variables like gender equality and religious attitudes. It extends terrorism research by including both domestic and transnational terrorism. It identifies country level factors of gender inequality and religiousness that influence terrorism experienced by a state in a certain year. It contributes to literature exploring impact of attitudes on terrorism, and also identifies important gaps between cultural attitudes and actual outcomes.

Like any cross national quantitative analysis this study is limited by data constraints with regard to generalizability of results to countries not included in the study and applicability of findings to countries with different socio-political, economic and cultural contexts. However various statistical controls are introduced in the study to control for these variations. Drawing panel data from various sources introduces numerous data constraints like the number of countries and years for which data is available. For instance for the time period of interest, the World Values Survey covers less countries than the Global Terrorism Database. World Values survey covers limited number of countries and some important countries with regard to high terrorism are missed. Standard limitations of survey data for World Values Survey might apply here like non-response and recall bias. These biases should be partially mitigated by the survey's sampling methods. There are also issues with multicollinearity and heteroskedasticity in the data. When possible these constraints are controlled for or corrected. More detail is provided in each of the following essays.

References:

Abadie, Alberto. (2006). Poverty, Political Freedom, and the Roots of Terrorism. *The American Economic Review, 96*(2), 50-56.

Alison, Miranda. (2004). Women as Agents of Political Violence: Gendering Security. *Security Dialogue, 35*(4), 447-463. doi: 10.1177/0967010604049522

Asal, Victor, & Rethemeyer, R. Karl. (2006). Researching Terrorist Networks. *Journal of Security Education, 1*(4), 65-74. doi: 10.1300/J460v01n04_06

Asal, Victor, & Rethemeyer, R. Karl. (2008). The Nature of the Beast: Organizational Structures and the Lethality of Terrorist Attacks. *Journal of Politics, 70*(2), 437-449.

Atran, Scott, & Ginges, Jeremy. (2012). RELIGIOUS AND SACRED IMPERATIVES IN HUMAN CONFLICT. *Science, 336*(6083), 855-857. doi: 10.2307/41584849

Belli, Roberta (2012). Financial Crime and Political Extremism in the U.S. University of Maryland.: The National Consortium for the Study of Terrorism and Responses to Terrorism (START)

Berko, Anat, & Erez, Edna. (2007). Gender, Palestinian Women, and Terrorism: Women's Liberation or Oppression? *Studies in Conflict & Terrorism, 30*(6), 493-519. doi: 10.1080/10576100701329550

Berman, Eli. (2009). *Radical, religious, and violent: the new economics of terrorism*: The MIT Press.

Bloom, Mia. (2005). *Dying to Kill*. New York: Columbia University Press.

Bloom, Mia. (2011). Bombshells: Women and Terror. *Gender Issues, 28*(1/2), 1-21. doi: 10.1007/s12147-011-9098-z

Burgoon, Brian. (2006). On Welfare and Terror: Social Welfare Policies and Political-Economic Roots of Terrorism. *The Journal of Conflict Resolution, 50*(2), 176-203.

Caiazza, Amy. (2001). Why gender matters in understanding September 11: Women, militarism, and violence *Publication no. 1908*. Washington, DC: Institute for Women's Policy Research.

Caprioli, Mary. (2000). Gendered Conflict. *Journal of Peace Research, 37*(1), 51-68.

Caprioli, Mary. (2003a). Gender Equality and Civil Wars: CPR Unit of the World Bank.

Caprioli, Mary. (2003b). Gender Equality and State Aggression: The Impact of Domestic Gender Equality on State First Use of Force. *International Interactions, 29*(3), 195.

Caprioli, Mary. (2005). Primed for Violence: The Role of Gender Inequality in Predicting Internal Conflict. *International Studies Quarterly, 49*(2), 161-178.

Caprioli, Mary, & Boyer, Mark A. (2001). Gender, Violence, and International Crisis. *The Journal of Conflict Resolution, 45*(4), 503-518.

Cook, David. (2005). Women Fighting in Jihad ? *Studies in Conflict & Terrorism, 28*(5), 375-384. doi: 10.1080/10576100500180212

Crenshaw, Martha. (1981). The Causes of Terrorism. *Comparative Politics, 13*(4), 379-399.

Crenshaw, Martha. (1989). *Terrorism and International Cooperation*: Institute for East-West Security Studies New York, NY.

Crenshaw, Martha. (2010). Thoughts on Relating Terrorism to Historical Contexts. In M. Crenshaw (Ed.), *Terrorism in Context*: Pennsylvania State University Press.

Cunningham, Karla J. (2003). Cross-Regional Trends in Female Terrorism. *Studies in Conflict & Terrorism, 26*(3), 171-195. doi: 10.1080/10576100390211419

Dreher, A., & Fischer, J.A.V. (2011). Does government decentralization reduce domestic terror? An empirical test. *Economics Letters, 111*(3), 223-225.

Enders, Walter, & Sandler, Todd. (2000). Is Transnational Terrorism Becoming More Threatening? A Time-Series Investigation. *The Journal of Conflict Resolution, 44*(3), 307-332.

Enders, Walter, & Sandler, Todd. (2002). Patterns of Transnational Terrorism, 1970-1999: Alternative Time-Series Estimates. *International Studies Quarterly, 46*(2), 145-165.

Enders, Walter, Sandler, Todd, & Gaibulloev, Khusrav. (2011). Domestic versus transnational terrorism: Data, decomposition, and dynamics. *Journal of Peace Research, 48*(3), 319-337. doi: 10.1177/0022343311398926

Eubank, William, & Weinberg, Leonard. (1994). Does democracy encourage terrorism? *Terrorism and Political Violence, 6*(4), 417-435.

Eubank, William, & Weinberg, Leonard. (2001). Terrorism and Democracy: Perpetrators and Victims. *Terrorism and Political Violence, 13*(1), 155-164. doi: 10.1080/09546550109609674

Fox, Jonathan. (2004). The Rise of Religious Nationalism and Conflict: Ethnic Conflict and Revolutionary Wars, 1945-2001. *Journal of Peace Research, 41*(6), 715-731. doi: 10.2307/4149714

Fox, Jonathan, & Sandler, Shmuel. (2004). *Bringing religion into international relations*: Cambridge Univ Press.

Friedman, Marilyn. (2008). Female Terrorists: What Difference Does Gender Make? *Social Philosophy Today, 23*, 189-200.

Galvin, Deborah M. (1983). The Female Terrorist: A Socio-Psychological Perspective. *Behavioral Sciences & the Law, 1*(2), 19-32.

Gentry, Caron E. (2009). Twisted Maternalism. *International Feminist Journal of Politics, 11*(2), 235-252. doi: 10.1080/14616740902789609

Gunawardena, Arjuna. (2006). Female black tigers: A different breed of cat? *Female suicide bombers: Dying for equality*, 81-90.

Hoffman, Bruce. (1995). "Holy terror": The Implications of Terrorism Motivated by a Religious Imperative. *Studies in Conflict & Terrorism, 18*(4), 271-284.

Hoffman, Bruce. (1999). *Inside Terrorism*. New York: Columbia University Press.

Hoffman, Bruce. (2006). *Inside Terrorism* (Second ed.). New York: Columbia University Press.

Huber, Wolfgang. (2011). Religion and violence in a globalised world. *Verbum et Ecclesia, 32*(2), 39-46. doi: 10.4102/ve.v32i2.581

Hudson, Valerie M. (2012). *Sex and world peace*. New York: Columbia University Press.

Hudson, Valerie M., Caprioli, Mary, Ballif-Spanvill, Bonnie, McDermott, Rose, & Emmett, Chad F. (2008). The Heart of the Matter: The Security of Women and the Security of States. *International Security, 33*(3), 7-45.

Iannaccone, Laurence R., & Berman, Eli. (2006). Religious extremism: The good, the bad, and the deadly. *Public Choice, 128*(1/2), 109-129. doi: 10.1007/s11127-006-9047-7

Jenkins, Brian Michael. (1980). The study of Terrorism: Definitional problems *The Rand paper series*. Santa Monica, California: RAND.

Juergensmeyer, Mark. (2001). Terror in the Name of God. *Current History, 100*(649), 357-361.

Juergensmeyer, Mark. (2003). *Terror in the mind of God : the global rise of religious violence* (Third ed.). Berkley and Los Angeles: University of California Press.

Kis-Katos, Krisztina, Liebert, Helge, & Schulze, Günther G. (2011). On the origin of domestic and international terrorism. *European Journal of Political Economy, 27*, S17-S36.

Krieger, Tim, & Meierrieks, Daniel. (2010). Terrorism in the worlds of welfare capitalism. *Journal of Conflict Resolution, 54*(6), 902-939.

Krueger, Alan B. (2008). *What makes a terrorist: economics and the roots of terrorism (New Edition)*: Princeton University Press.

Kunz, Rahel, & Sjoberg, Ann-Kristin. (2009). Empowered or Oppressed? Female Combatants in the Colombian Guerrilla: The Case of the Revolutionary Armed Forced of Colombia - FARC. *Conference Papers -- International Studies Association*, 1-33.

Kydd, Andrew H., & Walter, Barbara F. (2006). The Strategies of Terrorism. *International Security, 31*(1), 49-80.

LaFree, Gary, & Dugan, Laura. (2007). Introducing the Global Terrorism Database. *Terrorism & Political Violence, 19*(2), 181-204. doi: 10.1080/09546550701246817

Lai, Brian. (2007). 'Draining the Swamp': An Empirical Examination of the Production of International Terrorism, 1968-1998. *Conflict Management and Peace Science, 24*(4), 297-310. doi: http://cmp.sagepub.com/archive/

Li, Quan. (2005). Does Democracy Promote or Reduce Transnational Terrorist Incidents? *The Journal of Conflict Resolution, 49*(2), 278-297.

Li, Quan, & Schaub, Drew. (2004). Economic Globalization and Transnational Terrorism: A Pooled Time-Series Analysis. *The Journal of Conflict Resolution, 48*(2), 230-258.

McCormick, Gordon H. (2003). TERRORIST DECISION MAKING. *Annual Review of Political Science, 6*(1), 473-507.

Melander, Erik. (2005). Gender Equality and Intrastate Armed Conflict. *International Studies Quarterly, 49*(4), 695-714.

Midlarsky, Manus I., Crenshaw, Martha, & Yoshida, Fumihiko. (1980). Why Violence Spreads: The Contagion of International Terrorism. *International Studies Quarterly, 24*(2), 262-298.

Nacos, Brigitte L. (2005). The Portrayal of Female Terrorists in the Media: Similar Framing Patterns in the News Coverage of Women in Politics and in Terrorism. *Studies in Conflict & Terrorism, 28*(5), 435-451. doi: 10.1080/10576100500180352

Ness, Cindy D. (2005). In the Name of the Cause: Women's Work in Secular and Religious Terrorism. *Studies in Conflict & Terrorism, 28*(5), 353-373. doi: 10.1080/10576100500180337

Newman, Edward. (2006). Exploring the "root causes" of terrorism. *Studies in Conflict & Terrorism, 29*(8), 749-772.

O'Rourke, Lindsey A. (2009). What's Special about Female Suicide Terrorism? *Security Studies, 18*(4), 681-718. doi: 10.1080/09636410903369084

Oberschall, Anthony. (2004). Explaining terrorism: The contribution of collective action theory. *Sociological Theory, 22*(1), 26-37.

Piazza, James A. (2008). Incubators of Terror: Do Failed and Failing States Promote Transnational Terrorism? *International Studies Quarterly, 52*(3), 469-488.

Ranstorp, Magnus. (1996). Terrorism in the Name of Religion. *JOURNAL OF INTERNATIONAL AFFAIRS-COLUMBIA UNIVERSITY, 50*, 41-62.

Regan, Patrick M., & Paskeviciute, Aida. (2003). Women's Access to Politics and Peaceful States. *Journal of Peace Research, 40*(3), 287.

Robison, Kristopher K. (2010). Unpacking the Social Origins of Terrorism: The Role of Women's Empowerment in Reducing Terrorism. *Studies in Conflict & Terrorism, 33*(8), 735-756. doi: 10.1080/1057610x.2010.494171

Sánchez-Cuenca, Ignacio, & de la Calle, Luis. (2009). Domestic Terrorism: The Hidden Side of Political Violence. *Annual Review of Political Science, 12*(1), 31-49.

Sandler, Todd. (2003). Collective action and transnational terrorism. *The World Economy, 26*(6), 779-802.

Satana, Nil S, Inman, Molly, & Birnir, Jóhanna Kristín. (2013). Religion, Government Coalitions, and Terrorism. *Terrorism and Political Violence, 25*(1), 29-52.

Schmid, Alex. (1992). The response problem as a definition problem. *Terrorism and Political Violence, 4*(4), 7-13. doi: 10.1080/09546559208427172

Schmid, Alex. (2004). TERRORISM -- THE DEFINITIONAL PROBLEM. *Case Western Reserve Journal of International Law, 36*(2/3), 103-147.

Schmid, Alex, & Jongman, Albert. (1988). *Political Terrorism*. New Brunswick, NJ: Transaction.

Schweitzer, Yoram. (2006). *Female suicide bombers: dying for equality?* : Jaffee Center for Strategic Studies, Tel Aviv University.

Sjoberg, Laura. (2010). Introduction. In L. Sjoberg (Ed.), *Gender and international security : feminist perspectives*. London, UK, New York Routledge.

Speckhard, Anne. (2008). The Emergence of Female Suicide Terrorists. *Studies in Conflict & Terrorism, 31*(11), 1023-1051. doi: 10.1080/10576100802408121

Stack, Alisa. (2011). Zombies versus Black Widows. In L. Sjoberg & C. E. Gentry (Eds.), *Women, Gender, and Terrorism*. Athens and London: The University of Georgia Press.

Teorell, Jan, Nicholas Charron, Marcus Samanni, Sören Holmberg & Bo Rothstein. (2011). The Quality of Government Dataset. Retrieved January 12, 2012, from University of Gothenburg: The Quality of Government Institute http://www.qog.pol.gu.se

Tickner, J. Ann. (1992). *Gender in international relations : feminist perspectives on achieving global security* New York Columbia University Press.

Urdal, Henrik. (2006). A clash of generations? Youth bulges and political violence. *International Studies Quarterly, 50*(3), 607-629.

Von Knop, Katharina. (2007). The Female Jihad: Al Qaeda's Women. *Studies in Conflict & Terrorism, 30*(5), 397-414. doi: 10.1080/10576100701258585

Weinberg, Leonard, & Eubank, William. (2011). Women's Involvement in Terrorism. *Gender Issues, 28*(1/2), 22-49. doi: 10.1007/s12147-011-9101-8

White, Jonathan R. . (2012). *Terrorism and Homeland Security* (7th ed.): Wadsworth, Cengage Learning

World Values Survey (2000). from World Values Survey Association

Chapter 2: Why her voice matters: The impact of Women's Rights on how States experience Terrorism

2.1 Introduction

Terrorism is gendered in the manner it is produced, perpetuated, experienced, countered and deterred. Looking at various factors that predict terrorism in a country, this essay examines whether women's rights have an impact on how much terrorism a country experiences. This study is a cross-national time series quantitative analysis of women's rights as predictors of terrorism, using data from the Global Terrorism Database (GTD) (LaFree & Dugan, 2007) for 155 countries from 1981-2002. Looking at both domestic and transnational terrorism I find that women's political empowerment is a significant predictor of whether a state experiences terrorism.

None of the empirical studies on the topic so far have investigated the impact of gender inequality on domestic terrorism. A state can experience both domestic and transnational terrorism. Domestic terrorism involves perpetrators, victims and audiences from just the host or base country, while international or transnational terrorism involves more than one country (Enders & Sandler, 2002; Enders et al., 2011)[1].

The results show that women's political empowerment may be a contributing factor to reducing terrorism. This is different from Robison's finding that women's economic empowerment deters terrorism. Perhaps this is because Robison (2010) does

---

[1] Detailed discussion on domestic and transnational terrorism is included in Chapter1- Introduction to this dissertation

not include domestic terrorism and limits his analysis to only transnational terrorism. This paper fills that gap, looks at domestic and transnational terrorism separately and finds evidence that domestic gender equality affects domestic terrorism more than transnational terrorism. In addition this paper extends the analysis by looking at the regime type in states, finding that women in parliament have a greater impact on lowering terrorism in democracies rather than in dictatorships. This paper argues that women's collective political agency needs to be recognized and supported for sustainable peace and stability. The results have significant policy implications, suggesting that increasing women's voices in parliaments and other higher decision-making bodies effectively curbs terrorism.

This study is important especially given the growing emphasis on promoting gender equality as a strategy for sustainable peace and security by many international organizations and policy makers (Anderlini, 2000; Mazurana, Raven-Roberts, & Parpart, 2005; UN, 2000). Many organizations including the United Nations, the United States Institute of Peace and the Women's International League for Peace and Freedom (WILPF)[2], advocate representation and inclusion of women in peacekeeping and conflict resolution, and conflict prevention in decision-making positions. The United States government has recently paid more attention to advancing women's rights as a counterterrorism strategy (Obama, 2010) and women's role in overall foreign policy goals[3]. One of the major lessons learned in the US-led war on terror is that over emphasis

---

[2] See United States Institute of Peace website, http://www.usip.org/issue-areas/women
See Women's International League for Peace and Freedom (WILPF) website, http://wilpfus.org/
[3] Hillary Clinton: Empower girls and women (Accessed Oct 2012), available at

on militarized response to terrorism can be counterproductive (Hawkesworth, 2008; Höglund, 2003; Mohanty, 2003; Mohanty, Pratt, & Riley, 2008; Pillar, 2001; Sutton & Novkov, 2008). Further, there is growing acknowledgement that counterterrorism is not a war, but a struggle and a process, requiring long-term policy solutions.

Although gender equality is advocated as a counterterrorism strategy, empirical evidence that supports this strategy is sparse at best. Numerous case studies exist, but a cross sectional analysis of the issue is essential to make connections visible at the state level. This study provides robust evidence of the critical link between women's political participation and decrease in terrorism. There is growing literature exploring the links between gender and political violence (Caprioli, 2000, 2003a, 2003b, 2005; Hudson, 2012; Hudson et al., 2008; Melander, 2005) and gender and terrorism (Alison, 2003; Bloom, 2011; Cunningham, 2003; Dalton & Asal, 2011; Sjoberg & Gentry, 2007; Stack, 2011). However so far there is no systematic analysis of the key role of women's rights in predicting terrorism, especially domestic terrorism, at the state level. A review of the studies examining female involvement in terrorism shows that there is little quantitative research and more reliance on narrative rather than statistical analysis (Jacques & Taylor, 2009). There is a wealth of rich qualitative evidence at the individual and case study level exploring these multi-layered connections but in the absence of strong empirical evidence at the state level, these studies are unable to effect mainstream impact on state policies[4].

---

http://articles.cnn.com/2010-12-12/opinion/clinton.empower.girls_1_women-equal-rights-fairness-issue-cow?_s=PM:OPINION

[4] Hudson, Valerie M. (2012, April 24). 'What sex means for world peace', Foreign Policy. (Retrieved October 2012 from http://www.foreignpolicy.com/articles/2012/04/24/what_sex_means_for_world_peace?page=0,0

There is evidence that countries with fewer women's rights experience more political violence and conflict. The central claim of this paper is that women's collective agency expressed through political power is an effective deterrent to terrorism. Agency means the ability to make effective life choices (Kabeer, 1999b). The World Development Report (2012) emphasizes that giving women a voice in matters that affect them and society at large is critical to building a peaceful society. There is evidence that one of the ways in which women's agency is actively demonstrated and collectively practiced is when they are politically empowered (WDR, 2012). Decision-making is an integral part of expressing agency. This study provides evidence that increases in women's political power provide them an effective avenue to express their agency in favor of peace, and thus diminishes threats of terrorism. At the same time it is imperative to acknowledge that agency is never independent of circumstances or the socio-political context within which individuals operate and make decisions. This study suggests that democracy provides more favorable circumstances for women to practice collective agency.

In the first section the paper focuses on the International Relations and Feminist Security Studies literature exploring the link between gender relations and state levels of violence. The second section presents the research design, discussion on dependent and independent variables and the results. The third section concludes with the interpretations and thoughts for future research.

2.2 Literature Review

The sheer absence of women from the dominant discourse on war, violence and terrorism makes it worth investigation. By asking 'Where are the women?' Cynthia Enloe (1990) in her seminal work 'Bananas, Beaches, and Bases' triggered a feminist investigation into the construction of war and political violence as gender neutral. Women are made invisible in masculinist narratives that obscure the multiple roles women play in war and political violence. In these narratives, women are portrayed only as passive victims or silent supporters of men's decisions to wage wars and perpetuate violence (Cockburn, 1999; Kaufman & Williams, 2007). Feminist scholars challenge masculinist narratives of war and violence that are based on andocentric assumptions, which hide the multiple and complex relations gender has with war, political violence and terrorism (Enloe, 1983, 1990, 2007; Hawkesworth, 2008; Mohanty et al., 2008). Feminists argue that gender is a social construction of ideas, assumptions, roles, relationships and stereotypes ascribed to men and women on the basis of their biological sex (Tickner, 1992; West & Don, 1987). A gender perspective entails acknowledging women's experiences, recognition of gender-based exclusion in decision-making positions, and questioning women's invisibility in international theory and practice (Blanchard, 2003; Caprioli, 2004; Caprioli, Emmett, Hudson, Spanvill, & McDermott, 2007; Enloe, 2007; Regan & Paskeviciute, 2003).

The current literature looking at conditions and determinants of terrorism focuses on characteristics of states that make them likely targets of terrorism. Conventional and dominant discourse on international terrorism looks at various predictors of terrorism for a country. These include political system, regime type, economic variables such as gross domestic product (GDP) per capita, trade, military expenditure, size of state and population (Abadie, 2006; Braithwaite & Li, 2007; Burgoon, 2006; Enders & Sandler, 2002; Feldmann & Pera la, 2004; Freytag, Krüger, Meierrieks, & Schneider, 2011; Li, 2005; Li & Schaub, 2004; Piazza, 2006, 2008a, 2011).

Since the terrorist attacks of 11 September 2001, there has been increased and passionate interest in exploring the complex relationships and links between terrorism and gender (Caiazza, 2001; Höglund, 2003; Hunt & Rygiel, 2006; Thobani, 2007). Even though the relation between gender and terrorism is not a new phenomenon[5] (Bloom, 2005; Sjoberg, Cooke, & Neal, 2011; Speckhard, 2008), contemporary feminist scholarship studying war, violence and terrorism continues to be located outside conventional International Relations discourse (Caprioli, 2004; Hudson et al., 2008; Runyan & Peterson, 1991; Sjoberg, 2009; Steans, 2003; Tickner, 1992, 1997; Zalewski, 1993).

Feminist critiques of the mainstream discourse on terrorism reveal the absence of women's voices and experiences, and help identify an important research gap in the dominant discourse: Is gender inequality a predictor of terrorism? Dominant models examining terrorism have an inherent androcentric bias, where the problem, research design, definitions, relevant evidence, data collection, data analysis, and interpretation of

---

[5] Women's involvement in terrorist acts, insurgencies and movements is not a new phenomenon. There is evidence of their involvement in many terrorist organizations like Peru's Shining Path, IRA, al Qaeda, Liberation Tamil Tigers of Ealam (Sri Lanka), Kurdistan Worker's Party (Turkey), HAMAS (Palestine), Zapatistas (Mexico), Abu Syyaf (Philippines), Symbionese Liberation Army (United States), Taliban (Afghanistan), Revolutionary Armed Forces of Columbia (FARC). Also women have had leadership roles in Baader-Meinhof (Germany), Red Brigades (Italy), Front Line (Prima Linea) (Italy) ETA (Spain and France), Japanese Red Army, the People's Liberation Front for Palestine, the Chechen resistance movement, the Weather Underground (United States). Some organizations even proclaim commitment to gender equality as one of their revolutionary goals" (Taken from Gentry and Sjoberg, 2011, p59)

results are based on the erroneous assumption of a gender-neutral world. Feminist perspectives on terrorism equip us with analytical tools to unpack popular gendered stereotypes, incomplete understandings, and masculinist assumptions.

2.2.1 Gender and Terrorism

Different groups of women are positioned differently with regard to political violence and terrorism. There is substantial amount of research suggesting that women and men hold different understandings of peace, security, conflict resolution and the use of force, given their socially constructed gender identities and experiences (Elshtain, 1987; Enloe, 1990, 2007; Gilligan, 1982; Mazurana et al., 2005; Tickner, 1992). Women experience a disproportionate share of effects of armed violence and conflict with massive incidents of sexual and gender-based violence as weapons of war (Pankhurst, 2009; UN, 2004; WfWi, 2008, 2009, 2010). Although men are more likely to be directly involved with political violence and terrorism, women as easy targets and victims of political violence are often overlooked and underestimated (Caiazza, 2001; Pankhurst, 2009; Plümper & Neumayer, 2006).

In recent wars civilian deaths outnumber military ones, and women and children have become major causalities (Cockburn, 2001; Giles & Hyndman, 2004). They are victims of terrorism and political violence like men, but violence takes on an acutely gendered dimension when women are singled out for sexual violence, rape and prostitution. They also bear the consequences of being displaced by war, conflict and violence, losing family and at times they suffer simply by being helpless bystanders (Caiazza, 2001; Moser, 2001). Nevertheless, women are not just victims of war and political violence, as they enlist increasing numbers in the military as combatants (Goldstein, 2003; Höglund, 2003). But with men in higher decision-making positions, the gendered assignment strategies in the military tend to propel women into non-combat duties such as military prisons, and prefer men for combat duties and frontline soldiering[6] (Detraz, 2012; Enloe, 1983, 2007).

As non-combatants, women are more likely to support peace not because they are biologically or inherently more pacifistic, but because women survivors bear relatively higher burdens and costs of armed-conflict and the post-conflict period. Women are direct victims of violence (including sexual violence[7]), disease, breakdown of social structures and lack of health care. They are also primary caretakers of those who are injured, sick, orphaned, abused, displaced or otherwise impacted by armed conflict (UN, 2004; WfWi, 2008, 2009, 2010). Their multiple roles as caregivers, survivors, providers, recoverers, supporters, mediators and peace-builders in post-conflict and war periods challenges the dichotomy of men as protector and combatant, and women as mere victims. It draws attention to their agency as non-combatants and survivors of violence.

While contemplating issues of gender inequality and terrorism we need to be cautious of slipping into essentialist concepts of gender, with stagnant assumptions of

---

[6] Only recently the US military has allowed women in combat roles and it is still too early to comment on how this policy will be implemented. See Domi, Tanya L. (2013, February 8). 'Women in Combat: Policy Catches Up With Reality'. The New York Times. Retrieved February 20, 2013 from http://www.nytimes.com/2013/02/09/opinion/women-in-combat-policy-catches-up-with-reality.html?_r=0

[7] UN estimates that about 250,000 to 500,000 women were raped in Rwandan genocide, between 20,000 to 50,000 women were raped in Bosnia and Herzegovina, at least 50,000 women were victims of sexual violence in Sierra Leone, and in Democratic Republic of the Congo an estimated 200,000 women and girls were raped. These figures are estimated numbers as rape is under-reported due to social stigma and in times of conflict the mechanisms to gather such information are broken (for further information see http://www.womenwarpeace.org/docs/drc_archive.pdf).

peaceful women and aggressive men. In popular imagination pacifist imagery is associated with femininity (Höglund, 2003; Hudson et al., 2008) leading to gendered norms and images of conflictual men and cooperative women (Caprioli, 2003b). Biologically deterministic cultural norms associate women with their reproductive role as caregiver, and it is seen as 'normal' or 'natural' that they should be peaceful and nurturing based on their biology. Feminists contest this simplistic notion and argue that women engaging or not engaging in terrorist acts are stigmatized with gendered stereotypes and clichés (Gentry & Sjoberg, 2011; Nacos, 2005).

The simplistic analysis of associating women with peace serves to disempower women by denying them agency and voice (Sjoberg et al., 2011; Sjoberg & Gentry, 2007; Tickner, 2001). Sjoberg and Gentry (2007) argue that many previous studies of women and terrorism portray women either as silent and helpless victims, sacrificing mothers, crazy and irrational deviants, fanatical contenders or heartless whores. A female terrorist is labeled as 'a slut, a demon, a vulgar slap-in-the-face to all that femininity is supposed to be' (Stack, 2011). This assessment reflects a sexist attitude which generates the notion that 'terrorism is not women's work' (Cooper, 1979). These studies fail to capture the notion that women, like men, are capable of choosing violence or peace in a given situation.

There is a long history of women's involvement in terrorism (Bloom, 2011; Cook, 2005) and there is growing evidence of women playing a significant role in terrorist organizations in Israel/Palestinian territories, Sri Lanka, Chechnya, Turkey, Jordan, India and Iraq (Berko & Erez, 2007; Speckhard, 2008; Von Knop, 2007). In fact the popular notions of feminine pacifism makes female terrorism highly unanticipated, underestimated and thus highly effective (Bloom, 2005; Cunningham, 2003; Dalton & Asal, 2011; Von Knop, 2007). Contrary to popular belief that women join terrorist organizations due to coercion or use of force, studies show that women engage in terrorism on a voluntary basis, expressing their agency (Alison, 2004; Parashar, 2011). Feminist scholars contend that female terrorists lead complex lives, which are both full of agency and also fraught with constraints on that agency. Be it the role of victim, facilitator, perpetuator or peace keeper, ignoring women's agency seriously limits and distorts our understanding of the relationship between gender and terrorism.

Current literature on gender and state violence suggests that women's security is related to a state's security. Hudson et al. (2008) argue that gender relations affect the way violence is experienced by states, because of the construction of masculinity and patriarchal norms practiced there (Hudson et al., 2008). Caprioli (2000) found that domestic gender equality has a pacifying effect on state behavior at the international level. Research suggests that more gender equality decreases international conflict (Caprioli, 2000, 2003b; Caprioli & Boyer, 2001; Melander, 2005) and reduces internal conflict (Caprioli, 2005). Research also suggests that societies based on norms of equality are more peaceful (Melander, 2005). Stretching the empirically tested gender-conflict results to explore the gender and terrorism relationship leads to the following hypothesis.

H1: Holding all else constant: Countries with higher gender equality experience less terrorism.

Even though some terrorist groups motivated by domestic grievances and concerns undertake international terrorism to attract greater attention (Enders et al., 2011), domestic terrorist incidents are far more in number and are more violent than transnational ones (Abadie, 2006; Enders et al., 2011; Sánchez-Cuenca & de la Calle, 2009). Domestic terrorism is less visible since more media attention is awarded to international terrorism. Not all terrorist organizations have the resources and capacity to carry out international attacks. It is relatively easier for terrorist organizations to carry out domestic, rather than transnational attacks, making domestic terrorism a more pervasive threat to the security of countries.

We can stretch the gender equality and state levels of terrorism argument while examining predictors of domestic terrorism. There is no research so far examining gender equality as predictor of domestic terrorism. We can hypothesize that the state level characteristics, including gender equality, directly influence levels of domestic terrorism.

H2: Countries with higher gender equality experience less domestic terrorism.

Women, even those involved in terrorist organizations, are not passive subjects but are active actors and are free agents making their own choices[8] (Alison, 2003, 2004; Parashar, 2011; Sjoberg et al., 2011; Stack, 2011). Women's rights are framed, experienced and practiced in a particular socio-economic and political context. In this respect the economic, social and political characteristics of a country need to be considered while studying these relationships and choices.

---

[8] Studying female terrorists in Liberation Tigers of Tamil Eelam (LTTE) Alison (2003) explains that there is no such thing as completely free or pure agency, as all individuals are influenced, constrained and impacted by the structures, institutions and discourses of their societies. It is important to see women's agency within the framework of 'relational autonomy' where choices are dependent on the gendered social and political context.

2.2.2 Terrorism and Economic Development

Looking at state factors that predict terrorism Bravo and Dias (2006) find that countries with a low Human Development Index (HDI) experience a higher number of terrorist attacks, implying a link between deprivation as a cause of terrorism. It is interesting to note that very few cross-national studies have found connections between economic inequality, poverty and terrorism (Brockhoff, Krieger, & Meierrieks, 2010; Krieger & Meierrieks, 2011).

Nevertheless with regard to terrorism research shows that country's Organization for Economic Co-operation and Development (OECD) membership is robustly associated with terrorism (Gassebner & Luechinger, 2011; Li & Schaub, 2004). The OECD countries are rich and influential and have high levels of economic development compared to non-OECD countries.

There is evidence that gender equality and economic development are positively related (Chen, 2004). With regard to gender equality Inglehart and Norris (2003) found that higher human development and societal modernization facilitate and boost equal opportunities for women. Finding relationship between gender equality and terrorism in countries with higher economic development leads to the following hypothesis:

H3: Gender equality has a stronger impact on lowering terrorism in countries with higher economic development.

Some studies present counterarguments to economic development as a predictor of terrorism. They argue that poorer countries are not at a higher risk of terrorist attack once country-specific characteristics like political freedom are taken into account (Abadie, 2006). Research is emerging to show that terrorism is not just a product of economic deprivation, or changes brought about by globalization or modernization. It is in fact a result of the national political dynamics and environment (Eubank & Weinberg, 2001; Lai, 2007b; Li, 2005; Weinberg & Eubank, 2011).

2.2.3 Terrorism and Political Environment

Linked to the political environment argument, studies suggest that advances in women's rights materialize when the quality of democracy is good. Looking at countries in Latin America, Htun (2003) asserts that political democratization is an important prerequisite for advancement of women's rights. Bjarnegård and Melander (2011) suggest that more democratic societies are more peaceful only if they have some minimum gender equality[9]. On the other hand research also shows that democratization does not always translate into women's rights and inclusiveness (Walsh, 2011).

This thesis argues that the concept of agency provides a framework for understanding the connection between democracy, gender equality and peace. Democratic societies are more peaceful if women have the agency to express their voice in matters of peace and war[10]. Overall, women are under-represented in parliaments in democracies even though they have long had a right to vote (Towns, 2010). Low representation of women in the parliaments is a basic deficit in representation itself. Studies suggest that a culture of peace would be promoted by gender equality in the

---

[9] However, Bjarnegård and Melander (2011) do not explain how to define or operationalize the term 'minimum gender equality'. They argue that democracy can facilitate peace only in interaction with political gender equality whereas militarized masculinity has a debilitating effect on peace.
[10] There is evidence that over time democracy creates favorable conditions for gender equality but the mix of factors affecting the number of female legislators varies depending on the length of the democratic experience of the country. In countries with a shorter time of democracy, the voting system explained the proportion of women in parliament, while in established democracies; the egalitarian conception of gender was significant in explaining those numbers. See (Beer, 2009; Tremblay, 2007; Walsh, 2011)

political apparatus of states (Caprioli & Boyer, 2001; Regan & Paskeviciute, 2003). The United Nations asserts that women must constitute 30% of 'critical mass' in the national legislatures in order to have a meaningful influence in decision-making processes ((DAW), 2005; (UNDP), 1995). Women's effectiveness in public forum improves as their proportional strength in numbers increases (Agarwal, 2010). Numbers do matter; surveys show that the higher the number of women in the parliament, the easier it is to address women's issues. In fact policy tools like quotas have had positive effect in this regard (Ballington, 2008). As of October 2012, on average women constitute only 20.2 % of national legislatures worldwide ((IPU), 2012).

Karl (1995) argues that women's effective political participation should include promoting gender equality, gaining control over one's life, building capacity for participating in decisions that affect one's life leading to transformative action. Political participation can be defined as effective involvement in the formulation and implementation of public policy at all levels of society, i.e. community, local, national, and international (Miranda, 2005). Perhaps most importantly, women in positions of power can influence decisions about war and peace (Tickner 1992). Koch and Fulton (2011) argue that increasing women's legislative representation decreases state conflict behavior and defense spending[11]. Another argument in favor of increasing the number of women in the parliament is that Bjarnegård and Melander (2011) assert that male

---

[11] Sutton, Morgen and Novkov (2008) mention Jeannette Rankin as an example of women legislators opposing war. She was the first female elected to the House of Representatives in 1916, and cast one out of 49 votes against US entering the World War I. She was the only one to vote against declaring war on Japan after the Pearl Harbor attack. Similarly Barbara Lee was the only member of congress in 2001, to vote against Authorization for Use of Military Force Against Terrorists (AUMF) in spite of intense public emotions and mobilization in favor of the war on terror. See Sutton and Novkov (2008) p 57.

dominated parliaments are more likely to get involved in intrastate-armed conflict and support use of violence. Parliaments with more women do not necessarily mean that only women support peace, but they do seem to support an environment where man can also vote for peaceful means of conflict resolution. Thus I hypothesize that:

H4: Gender equality has a stronger and negative impact on terrorism in democracies, rather than dictatorships.

Furthermore terrorism is strongly associated with local grievances and repressive regimes that terrorist organizations aspire to change (Hoffman & McCormick, 2004; McCormick, 2003). The local grievances are directly linked to domestic terrorism. Terrorist organizations need resources, including human capital; financial assets and technical expertise to engage in larger attacks and local grievances help boost local recruitment and social connections. (Sánchez-Cuenca & de la Calle, 2009).

A strong and vibrant democracy thrives on an inclusive parliament where local grievances and domestic inequalities can be discussed and addressed. Terrorists choose violence to attract attention and impress their audience in order to achieve their ideological goal (Asal & Rethemeyer, 2008b). Research shows that democracies make other avenues for protests available and discourage local grievances from escalating into conflict. The democratic political culture provides favorable climate to groups advancing women's rights. With regard to domestic gender inequality we can assume that it directly impacts domestic terrorism and has a stronger impact in democracies. Hence we hypothesize:

H5: Democratic countries with higher gender equality experience less domestic terrorism

So far there are very few empirical studies comparing domestic and transnational terrorism determinants, and none of them look at gender inequality as a predictor. Past studies on the topic have mostly used the International Terrorism: Attributes of Terrorist Events (ITERATE) or Institute for the Prevention of Terrorism (MIPT) Terrorism Knowledge Base datasets, which are limited to only international attacks (Enders & Sandler, 2000, 2002; Li, 2005; Li & Schaub, 2004; Piazza, 2008; Robison, 2010).

2.2.4 Domestic and Transnational Terrorism

As mentioned earlier, Robison analyzed domestic gender equality and its impact on transnational terrorism. However there is a debate that the causes of the two types of terrorism might be different. To check for state level explanations of terrorism, this study tested whether gender inequality has more effect on domestic or transnational terrorism, or both. With regard to gender inequality, which is a domestic issue, one can assume that it affects domestic terrorism more than transnational terrorism. This study uses a dataset developed by (Enders et al., 2011) which separates GTD incidents into domestic and international events[12]. Enders' et al. (2011) bifurcation of GTD dataset into domestic and transnational terror events has provided researchers the opportunity to conduct such an analysis and develop new insights.

---

[12] I will use dataset developed by (Enders et al., 2011), which separates domestic and international terrorist attacks in GTD. There are in GTD for 1970–2007, after applying three criteria: '(i) the attack is perpetrated for a political, socio- economic, or religious motive; (ii) the attack is intended to coerce, intimidate, or send a message to a wider audience than the immediate victim(s); and (iii) the attack is beyond the boundaries set by international humanitarian law' (Enders et al., 2011). The authors are left with 66,383 terrorist incidents to classify as domestic or transnational. Based on a five-step procedure, they list 12,862 transnational terrorist incidents; this number is similar to ITERATE which contains 12,784 transnational terrorist incidents for the same time interval. Whenever there is missing or unknown information the event is classified as unknown. So they determined 7,108 incidents as uncertain and identified 46,413 incidents as domestic incidents.

Transnational terrorism does not occur in a vacuum and has links to domestic terrorism. Terrorist groups weigh the operating costs both in the host and the target country. Operating costs include the socio-economic, political and cultural environment of a society. Aggregate country-specific factors impact terrorists' cost benefit matrices and their choice of target (Dreher & Fischer, 2011; Krieger & Meierrieks, 2011). Such determinants raise (or lower) the operating cost, causing decline (or increase) in terrorist activity (Lai, 2007a). With regard to the operating cost of the terrorist group I hypothesize that domestic gender equality would impact domestic terrorism more than transnational terrorism. Even though the direction of impact might be similar, given the different dynamics of the two kinds of terrorism the magnitude of impact would be different.

H6: Gender equality impacts domestic terrorism more than transnational terrorism

The following section explains the research design used to test the above-mentioned six hypotheses.

2.3 Research Design

This study is a quantitative analysis of the impact of gender inequality on incidents of terrorism using a panel data i.e. cross-national and time series, for 155 countries from 1981-2002. For this dataset maximum coverage is available for 1981-2002.

Dependent Variable

The dependent variable is a count of terrorist incidents experienced by a country in a single year. This data is based on Global Terrorism Database (GTD)[13], which is an open source database of domestic and transnational terrorist incidents occurring from 1970 to 2011, for more than 210 countries including disputed areas. GTD is a rich data source listing more than 104,000 cases and recording information for 15 categories of variables for each terrorist event. The three most comprehensive datasets on terrorism are ITERATE (Mickolus, 1984), MIPT dataset[14] and GTD. The ITERATE and MIPT datasets focus exclusively on transnational terrorism, while GTD is the most comprehensive and extensive dataset available on both domestic and transnational terrorist incidents worldwide. One of the major limitations of the dataset is that it is collected from open sources and bias can be introduced if an event is not reported[15].

Terrorism is a difficult and controversial term to define, with over a hundred scholarly or governmental definitions. This thesis employs the definitional criteria set up by the Global Terrorism Database (GTD) that an event must meet to be recorded as a terrorist attack. In this dataset there are four criteria: an event must be intentional; entail violence or the threat of it; is carried out by non-state actors; and is outside the context of legitimate warfare. In addition one of the two conditions should be met. Either the attack

---

[13] Available at: http://www.start.umd.edu/gtd

[14] The MIPT Terrorism Knowledge Base dataset was active from September 2004 to March 2008. Since 2009 another database is available called RAND Database of Worldwide Terrorism Incidents for domestic and transnational events from 1998 to present.

[15] The gender and state level terrorism relationship is complex and it is hard to establish a direct causal link due to lack of empirical research in this area. As with any quantitative analysis there are certain temporal and data constraints with this study, given the cross-sectional and time period data, and unreported and unclaimed attacks.

is carried out to influence a group larger than the immediate target, and/ or the act has a political, religious, social or ideological goal.

Independent Variable- Women's Rights

The key factor to have impact on terrorism is women's political power, so this study includes the percentage of women in parliament as an important variable measuring gender equality. The data on percentage of women in parliament/legislature is taken from (Melander, 2005) which is originally based on data from inter-parliamentary union. It covers 175 countries for a period from 1965 to 2002. If the parliament is bicameral, the number of women in upper house is used. This measure taps the voice women have in a society and captures their collective agency in that society.

There is consensus in scholarship that gender equality is a complex and multidimensional phenomenon (Kabeer, 2005). Measures of gender equality broadly include the social, political and economic rights that women have in a country. Along with the measure of women in parliament, this study also includes variables measuring women's economic and political rights provided by respective governments in the countries under consideration (Cingranelli & Richards, 2010). Both variables have a four value ordinal scale, where 0 represents no rights for women, 1 is for a few rights under law but poorly enforced by the government, 2 represents some rights enforced by government and 3 is coded for countries where all women's rights are guaranteed by law. These measures gauge the state support for women's rights. Given the above-mentioned discussion on gender equality and terrorism it is expected that these variables would be negatively related to terrorism. These variables provide valuable information about the different legal rights and protection extended to women by the concerned government. Women's social rights were not included because they are too closely correlated with women's economic rights.

Another variable of interest was women's literacy rate because female education is considered essential for female empowerment. However, it was not included for two reasons. First it was highly correlated with women's economic and social rights. Secondly in their study (Brockhoff et al., 2010) did not find any direct links between overall education and terrorism[16].

Rooted in the theoretical argument that political power is one of the important ways in which women express their agency, another critical variable that needs to be controlled is female leadership in a country. This dataset is also taken from (Melander, 2005) and covers 180 countries from 1965 to 2002[17]. A female leader is defined as the president, prime minister or any other decision maker of the last resort. This binary variable takes value (1) for female leader and (0) for male leader. Generally it would seem that women in highest decision-making positions reflect a society that values women. But it is observed that female leaders tend to adopt masculine behavior and decision-making attitudes in order to be taken seriously by their male colleagues. Although this variable has good coverage it is rarely 1.

The model includes 19 countries coded 1 that ever had a female leader. There are several examples of women in positions of power like Queen Elizabeth 1, Indira Ghandi,

---

[16] They found that education neither facilitates nor retards terrorism on its own, but may contribute to terrorism in poor political and socio-economic conditions, and decrease terrorism in favorable conditions.
[17] The original data is from (Caprioli & Boyer, 2001), extended by Melander (2005)

Golda Meir, Margaret Thatcher, Benazir Bhutto and Khalida Zia to name a few. It seems contradictory that these women made it to the top in a male-dominated and male-identified political environment. Johnson (2010) explains that 'patriarchy can accommodate a limited number of powerful women so long as the society retains its essential patriarchal character' (p 155). It is also observed that at times female leaders are more aggressive than men in crisis. A possible explanation given by scholars is that female leaders emulate male gender stereotypes to overcome stereotype of weakness associated with women in realpolitik issues of security, defense, war and economies (Alexander & Andersen, 1993; Sykes, 1993). A female leader does not mean that there is higher gender equality in a country instead she may have risen to this position through dynastic mechanisms (Melander, 2005). Given the character of this variable it can have a positive or negative sign depending on the regime of the country.

Other Controls

To control for omitted variable bias it is critical to employ important statistical controls when evaluating these relationships. Past studies show a variety of possible confounding causes of terrorism such as population, GDP per capita, measure of democracy, the number of conflicts a country has been involved in and a lagged variable for terrorism are predictors of terrorism. Population of a country is regarded as an important predictor of terrorist incidents (Braithwaite & Li, 2007; Burgoon, 2006; Lai, 2007a; Piazza, 2006). The data on population is taken from Quality of Government Dataset (Teorell, 2011), which is drawn from the Penn World Tables (Heston, Summers, & Aten, 2009). Studies have found that larger population makes it harder to police it, thus increasing the risk of terrorism (Eyerman, 1998). A larger population is likely to be a more heterogeneous population, making it easier for splinter groups to carry out terrorist attacks. A larger population is also a potential recruiting site for terrorist organizations and it increases monitoring costs for the government (Lai, 2007a). So the expected sign on the population coefficient is positive. On the other hand if a population is living in a democratic society there is less probability of violence as democratic culture provides space of public debate and dialogue. Therefore the population coefficient sign can be either positive or negative.

Studies have found that countries with more resources are better equipped to defend themselves against acts of terrorism, which makes them less attractive targets (Todd. Sandler & Lapan, 1988). For a measure of a country's resources the real GDP per capita variable is included in the model. The data is drawn from the Quality of Government Dataset (Teorell, 2011), based on the Penn World Tables (Heston et al., 2009). It is expected that the GDP variable would have a negative relationship with terrorism.

It is important to look at the level of democracy with regard to gender equality and peace (Bjarnegård & Melander, 2011; Walsh, 2011). Many past studies include some measure of democracy while studying terrorism (Braithwaite & Li, 2007; Eyerman, 1998; Li, 2005; Piazza, 2008a). The level of democracy in a country is drawn from the Quality of Government dataset and is based on the Polity IV dataset (Marshall & Jaggers, 2002). The scale of the 'Polity' variable ranges from 0 to 10 (with 10 being most democratic and 0 being least democratic). Like population, democracy can work both as a deterrent and as a potential trigger for terrorist incidents and affects a country in complex and multiple ways (Li, 2005). "…democratic participation reduces transnational terrorist incidents in a country, while government constraints increase the number of these incidents" (Li, 2005). Democratic societies have institutional constraints to curb terrorist attacks and it makes it easier for terrorist organizations to operate without being noticed due to freedom of movement and ideas (Crenshaw, 1981; Eubank & Weinberg, 1994, 2001; Ross, 1993; Wilkinson, 2011). Unlike democracies, military regimes can disregard civil liberties and effectively monitor terrorist organizations (Crenshaw, 1981; Li, 2005). Democratic participation reduces the need for organizations to resort to violent means for pursuit of goals. Therefore the sign on democracy coefficient can be either positive or negative.

To disaggregate data by regime type i.e. democracy and dictatorship, a dichotomous variable (called chga_demo) is employed. It is coded 1 if a country is a democracy and 0 if otherwise. This measure is developed by (Cheibub, Gandhi, & Vreeland, 2010)[18], who base their classification on minimalist criteria that citizens be periodically given the opportunity to choose their leaders by popular vote, and that multiple political parties are allowed to contest and are present within the legislature. Also, there is no consolidation of incumbent advantage such as unconstitutional closure of legislature or extension in incumbents' term by postponing elections. The transition years are coded as the regime that emerges in the previous year. This is a useful categorization to track changes in political regimes over time.

It can be argued that a dichotomous measure of democracy (i.e. chga_demo) may fail to capture the significant relationship between democracy and a dependent variable whereas a continuous measure may detect it. However using both democracy variables

---

[18] (Cheibub et al., 2010) are aware that there can be variations between democracies, with some countries being more democratic than the other but this classification is based on basic distinction between democracy and dictatorships, which is definite and non-interchangeable.

(i.e. Polity and chga_demo) would lead to multicollinearity, so one variable would have to be dropped[19].

Another important control variable for analyzing terrorist incidents is past incidents, which measure the history of terrorism in a country. There is evidence that if a country experiences a terrorist attack there is a higher probability of its experiencing future events. Terrorist organizations act by learning from each other, and imitating tactics (Braithwaite & Li, 2007; Midlarsky et al., 1980). Other studies examining the number of terrorist incidents in a state have found this variable to be significant (Braithwaite & Li, 2007; Lai, 2007a; Li, 2005; Li & Schaub, 2004). Empirical studies suggest a positive sign for the lagged incidents variable.

Literature suggests that if a country is involved in internal or international conflict, there is a significant possibility of a terrorist attack. So to control for the number of conflicts a target country is currently involved in, the data is coded from the UCDP/PRIO Armed conflict dataset (Gleditsch, Wallensteen, Eriksson, Sollenberg, & Strand, 2002), which is a count of the number of inter and intra state conflicts the country is involved in. Countries already involved in conflicts do not have sufficient resources to effectively defend its territories against terrorism (Lai, 2007a). Hence the expected sign for this variable is positive.

It is commonly believed that gender equality is related to the level of economic development of a country. To unpack the effect of economic development on terrorism and gender equality in a country, data is coded for countries by membership in OECD.

---

[19] I prefer using the 'chga_demo' variable when disaggregating my data by regime type given the benefit that it can be meaningfully interpreted. It is based on regime attributes that are distinct, identifiable and non-interchangeable. It is useful to know exactly the change that a political regime implies.

There are 34 member countries in OECD[20], which equals to 1 if a country belongs to OECD and 0 otherwise.

2.4 Estimation

This study employs pooled regression models using country-year data for 155 countries for the period 1981-2002. The years of the study are dictated by the years of data on the independent variable. One of the advantages of working with panel data is that we can control for changes over time and variations across countries. The unit of analysis is an individual country in a single year.

The dependent variable is a count variable i.e. the number of terrorist incidents experienced by a country in a single year. The GTD data comes in terror attack observation. By converting it to country-year format there are no observations for some country-years. To create a balanced panel, zeros are assigned to all countries and years without record. Given the nature of the dependent variable, an ordinary least square model can be inefficient, inconsistent and biased, so it is recommended to use models specifically designed for count outcomes (Long & Freese, 2006). The variance of the dependent variable is greater than the mean so we cannot use Poisson model (Long & Freese, 2006) (see Table 2.1). The more suitable probability model that fits this data is negative binomial. There are many country-year observations, which experience no attacks so the data on terror events is strongly skewed to the right leading to overdispersion (of zeros), which leads to underestimated standard errors. A negative

---

[20] For the list of countries see OECD website http://www.oecd.org/about/membersandpartners/

binomial model is typically used when the dependent variable is the raw count of terrorist attacks in a country-year format (Li, 2005; Li & Schaub, 2004; Midlarsky et al., 1980; Piazza, 2011; Robison, 2010; Robison, Crenshaw, & Jenkins, 2006; Walsh & Piazza, 2010). Robust standard errors are estimated, clustered by country to control for country specific variations. They are robust to cope with heteroskedasticity and serial correlation within any cross-sectional unit (Rogers, 1994; Williams, 2000).

The results for all incidents of terrorism are presented in Table 2.2, for domestic terrorism in Table 2.3 and transnational terrorism in Table 2.4. To test the hypotheses various models were estimated, disaggregating countries by wealth and regime type, to see the effects of gender equality on terrorism in economically developed and developing countries, and democratic and dictatorial regimes. The dichotomous democracy variable (chga_demo) was employed to disaggregate countries by regime type. As suspected it is highly correlated with the polity variable, with a value of 0.8427. To fix multicollinearity in the model, the polity variable was dropped while estimating those models.

For robustness check, logit regression is also estimated for whether a country suffered any terror attack, domestic and international in a given year. It is coded 1 for any attack and coded zero for no attack in the country in that year. The variable of women in parliament was statistically significant and consistently negative in all models[21].

The CIRI data on women's rights has an ordinal scale that may mask substantial differences across countries and years, and their effect on terrorism might be dramatically different. As a robustness check for women's economic and political rights, the author

---

[21] The results are available from author upon request

generated binary variables for the ordinal scale and tested the regressions using the binary variables. The percentage of women in parliament was statistically significant in all the models. None of the CIRI binary variables were statistically significant.

2.5 Interpretation

According to results in 2.2 for overall terrorism it is found that the women in parliament variable is consistently negative and statistically significant in all models. A 1% increase in women in parliament leads to a 5.9% decrease in terrorism (see Table-2.2, Model 3).

On average the percentage of women in parliament increases by 3.7 percentage points during an election cycle. With a 3.7% increase in women in parliament there is an approximate 20% decrease in terrorism. For 1981-2002, on average a country faced 10 attacks per year, so if there were a 3.7 point increase in percentage of women in parliament it would lead to 2 fewer terror attacks for that country in a particular year. These results in Table-2.2 support Hypothesis-1 that countries with higher gender equality experience less terrorism. These results suggest in Table-2.2 that the level of women's rights helps determine the likelihood of a country being attacked. It also implies that states with more male dominated parliaments are at a higher risk of terrorism.

Some scholars argue that the number of women in parliament is not a good indicator of level of women's rights. For instance the number of women in parliament is high in undemocratic countries like Rwanda and Cuba, where women might not have the same influence as in democracies. To test the difference in impact in democracies and dictatorships, models 6 and 7 in Table-2.2 show that a 1% increase in women in parliament leads to about 7% decrease in terrorism if country is democratic and about 4 % if it is otherwise. This confirms Hypothesis-4 that gender equality has stronger impact on terrorism in democratic societies than dictatorships.

In Table-2.3 for domestic terrorism the percentage of women in parliament has a negative and significant impact, confirming Hypothesis-2 that countries with higher gender equality experience less domestic terrorism (see Table-2.3, Models 1 to 9). Comparison of results between Table-2.3, Models 4 & 5 support Hypothesis-5, which implies that for domestic terrorism gender equality has greater impact in democratic societies than dictatorial regimes. The results suggest that for a 1% increase in women in parliament, domestic terrorism decreases by about 8% in democracies (Table-2.3, Model-4) and about 5% in dictatorships (Table-2.3, Model-5).

For transnational terrorism (see Table-2.4) the percentage of women in parliament is overall negative and significant except for dictatorial regimes (see Table 2.4- Model 5 & 8) where it is negative but not significant. Comparing domestic and transnational terrorism, all the results in Table-2.3 and Table-2.4 support Hypothesis-6 i.e. gender equality impacts domestic terrorism more than transnational terrorism. We see that a 1% increase in women in parliament lowers domestic terrorism by about 6.9 % (see Table-2.3, Model-1) and transnational terrorism by about 3.7% (see Table-2.4, Model-1).

Contrary to Robison's findings that women's economic empowerment lowers terrorism, the results in Table-2.4, Model-1 suggest that the number of women in parliament has a negative and statistically significant effect on terrorism than women's economic empowerment. In his study Robison (2010) bundles all the countries together and assumes transnational terrorism to be representative of overall terrorism. So even though he finds women's economic empowerment as having an impact on terrorism, this study finds that it is in non-OECD countries and dictatorships rather than democracies where the impact of women's economic empowerment is negative and significant (see Table-2.4, Models 3, 5 & 8). The analysis shows that the number of women in parliament is a consistent and significant deterrent to transnational terrorism, except in dictatorships.

Testing Hypothesis-3 i.e. gender equality has a stronger impact on lowering terrorism in countries with higher economic development, the results show that in both OECD or non-OECD countries the percentage of women in parliament has significant and negative impact on overall terrorism (Table-2.2, Model 4 & 5), on domestic terrorism (Table-2.3, Model 2 & 3) and transnational terrorism (Table-2.4, Model 2 & 3). The comparison of results between OECD and non-OECD countries in all three tables shows that women in parliament are more effective in OECD than non-OECD countries. For overall terrorism, a 1 % increase in this variable in OECD countries leads to about 6% decrease in terrorism compared to 4% decrease in non-OECD countries. On average in an election cycle the percentage of women in parliament increases by 3.2% in OECD countries and 3.9% in non-OECD countries. For 1981-2002, on average an OECD country faced 16 attacks per year. If there is about 3 point increase in women in parliament it leads to 2 fewer terror attacks for that country in a particular year. Non-OECD countries faced 9.9 attacks per year in the period 1981-2002. If there is a 3.9 point increase in women in parliament it leads to 1.58 fewer terror attacks for that country in a particular year. The results have a similar pattern for domestic and transnational events in OECD and non-OECD countries in Table-2.2 and Table-2.3.

Generally in all three tables the signs of the control variables, i.e. population, real GDP/ Capita, past incidents and conflicts, are the expected ones and are correlated in the hypothesized manner. In the base models (Table-2.2, Model 1& 2) polity is significant and positively related to terrorism. Coefficient on polity behaves similarly for domestic and transitional terrorism (see Table-2.3, Model-1 & Table-2.4, Model-1). This suggests that democracies are juicer targets for terrorists than dictatorships. Studies suggest that countries which afford their citizens basic civil liberties and political rights are more exposed to terrorist attacks (Eubank & Weinberg, 1994; Pape, 2003; Wade & Reiter, 2007). It was expected that women's economic and political rights variables would be negative but interestingly they are both negative and positive depending on the regime type. The female leadership variable is an interesting measure of women in power. In Table-2.2 it appears positive and significant at 1 percent for overall terrorism (see Table-2.2, Model-3), in Non-OECD (Table-2.2, Model-5), in democracies (Table-2.2, Model-6) and Non-OECD / democracies (Table-2.2, Model-10). Similarly in Table-2.3 it is positive and significant for domestic terrorism in all models except ones looking at OECD countries (Table-2.3, Model-2 & 6). For transnational terrorism it is positive and significant at a 10% level only in dictatorships (Table-2.4, Model-5). Data on female leaders are too sparse to draw any accurate statistical conclusions. The results however suggest that a lone woman in power is not a deterrent to terrorism. Compared to women in parliament we can conclude that there might be strength in numbers where women have opportunity to exercise their collective agency in decision-making.

2.6 Conclusion

This paper presents empirical evidence that gender equality, as measured by women in parliament, is a significant and strong predictor of whether a country will experience domestic and transnational terrorism. This study integrates literature from feminist security studies and finds empirical evidence that empowering women politically plays a role in attenuating terrorism. These results have valuable significance for policymakers. Based on the results for 1981-2002, increasing percentage of women in the parliament by just 3.7 points would reduce terrorism by 2 fewer attacks for a country in a particular year.

This paper also demonstrates that domestic gender equality has a greater impact on domestic terrorism than transnational terrorism. Previous studies examine the influence of women's empowerment on transnational terrorism only (Robison 2010). Even though domestic terrorism is greater in number than transnational one, the author is not aware of any study that analyzes gender equality impact on domestic terrorism. The findings of this paper have important policy implications for including women voices in parliaments to control domestic terrorism. Another important contribution of this paper is that it examines whether gender equality is more effective in democracies or dictatorship. It is found that democracies, although an attractive target for terrorists, are better protected if they have higher numbers of women in the parliament. This could possibly reflect a society that recognizes and acknowledges equality of unequal groups and disadvantaged communities. Compared to dictatorships, democracies tend to provide better space and opportunity for women's political voice to be heard.

Political empowerment for women provides them an opportunity to have their own voice rather than being considered helpless and hapless victims who need protection. A possible explanation of these results is that when the number of women in parliament increases, their country is more likely to improve rule of law that, in turn, deters terrorist incidents (Choi, 2010). Women's agency needs to be acknowledged and their voice needs to be heard in matters that affect their lives and those around them. Assuming that women are helpless victims of political violence limits their agency, delegitimizes their voices, and drastically limits our policy options to build peace and security. Despite limitations, persistent difficulties and lack of access to equal political participation faced by women in all countries, women's political participation has a significant impact on dampening terrorism.

It can be argued that many countries adopt quotas for women in parliament and it is thus not a good proxy for gender equality in the society. However quotas also suggest that these countries have recognized the need for temporary measures to bolster women's rights, and to address the historical disadvantages that create gender inequalities[22]. Including women in political decision-making is critical for challenging gendered norms, roles and relations that tend to reinforce, regenerate and reinscribe patterns of gender inequality. Empowerment entails a process of changing deeply held personal biases, attitudes, practices, structures and institutions (Akerkar, 2001; Kabeer, 1999a, 1999b). It is women's own voices in the society that can best reflect, question, challenge, protest,

---

[22] Both the Beijing Platform for Action (Pfau-Effinger) (1995) and the Convention on the Elimination of All Forms of Discrimination Against Women (CEDAW) (1997) recommend that governments must adopt quotas as temporary special measures to enhance the number of women in both appointive and elective positions in local and national levels of government.

negotiate and revisit the notions and practices of gender inequality. Their political participation is critical to initiating a cultural change in the attitudes, norms and practices that cultivate and reproduce women's subordination and other kinds of inequalities.

An important caveat to these results is to be aware of who empowers women and how they are empowered politically. Incorporating gender in understanding international security requires first to dismantle the flawed assumption of women being voiceless and second to deconstruct universalist notions of feminism (Mohanty, 2003). It means that the voice of the subaltern has to be acknowledged, recognized, heard and valued. Imposing collective speech to women from different races, geographic and historical locations assumes a cultural solidarity of a heterogeneous group of individuals. It creates a dependency of the 'subaltern' to have someone else speak for him/her (Spivak, 1988). Increasing the number of women in parliament does not automatically translate into equal participation, but it is an integral step to establish and promote a culture of equality and to afford space for women to express their collective political agency.

This realization reinforces the need for better information and data, robust investigation and rigorous research to explore the layers of complexity of how gender equality and terrorism intersect within a particular context. There is pressing need to consolidate data on how terrorism, war, conflict and political violence affect women and girls. Assuming that political violence is gender neutral, and that it does not have differential effects on men and women, distorts our understanding and gravely limits our policy solutions and alternatives[23].

---

[23] This paper demonstrates how domestic gender relations have an impact on state levels of terrorism. This relationship can have significant policy implications as countries with poor gender equality indicators could be potential green houses for terrorist organizations to breed and flourish. It is important to see whether attitudes towards gender equality facilitate or hinder terrorist organizations to form networks amongst themselves. The GTD data is based on location of the terror attack, for transnational terrorism further research needs to also explore gender equality impact by nationality of perpetuator to examine the connections and linkages of how domestic gender equality impacts international terrorism. More research is needed to understand the gendered power relations within the terrorist organization. Also how state policies of gender discrimination and patriarchal institutions impact the growth and proliferation of terrorist organizations in a country. Future research can analyze the length of experience; the level of female participation in parliament and the counter terrorism policies legislated. Also there is need to look at nature and structure of electoral institutions to better understand electoral system effects, on women's political participation and how it impacts the incidents of political violence.

Table 2.1: Descriptive statistics of variables in country-year format for 155 countries (1981-2002)

Variables	Mean	Standard Deviation
Terrorist Incidents	10.77	43.72
Domestic terrorism	7.41	34.32
Transnational terrorism	1.57	5.93
Women in parliament %	10.55	8.88
Women's economic rights	1.33	0.63
Women's political rights	1.68	0.67
Female leadership	0.0248	0.16
Population (thousands)	28391.24	113373.9
Real GDP/capita	9379.53	10609.26
Polity	5.64	3.48
Past Incidents	11.10	44.90
Conflict	0.31	0.73

Negative binomial regression of terrorist attack counts on economic and political independent variables
(...02)

	Model 1	Model 2	Model 3	Model 4 OECD	Model 5 Non OECD	Model 6 Democracy	Model 7 Dictatorship	Model 8 OECD/ Democracy	Model 9 OECD/ Dictatorship	Model Non O Democ
			-0.061*** (0.010)	-0.062*** (0.014)	-0.044*** (0.012)	-0.075*** (0.013)	-0.049*** (0.015)	-0.056*** (0.015)	-0.376*** (0.033)	-0.053* (0.018)
		-0.085 (0.155)	-0.101 (0.152)	0.242 (0.297)	-0.324** (0.150)	-0.071 (0.191)	-0.257 (0.199)	0.235 (0.278)	8.492*** (1.291)	-0.338* (0.167)
		-0.088 (0.159)	0.211 (0.174)	-0.488** (0.236)	0.209 (0.191)	0.121 (0.169)	0.344 (0.320)	-0.499** (0.234)	Omitted	0.255 (0.178)
		0.651** (0.311)	0.890*** (0.323)	0.255 (0.499)	1.134*** (0.335)	0.941*** (0.344)	1.538 * (0.784)	0.162 (0.446)	Omitted	1.369* (0.402)
	2.65e-06 (2.93e-06)	2.49e-06 (2.47e-06)	2.09e-06 (1.08e-06)	0.00001 (6.74e-06)	1.45e-06* (7.35e-07)	1.38e-06 (3.41e-06)	1.76e-06** (7.54e-07)	0.00001* (5.97e-06)	-0.0001*** (0.00002)	-1.79e (1.20e
	.00001* (9.39e-06)	-0.00001 (0.00001)	9.47e-06 (0.00001)	-0.000032 (0.00003)	-3.53e- (0.00002)	0.00003* (0.00002)	-2.31e-06 (0.00002)	-0.00003 (0.00003)	-0.008*** (0.001)	0.0000 (0.000
	.122*** 0.029)	0.146*** (0.038)	0.115*** (0.040)	0.104 (0.200)	0.107*** (0.041)					
	.0260*** 0.005)	0.024*** (0.004)	0.021*** (0.004)	0.024*** (0.005)	0.018*** (0.004)	0.019*** (0.004)	0.031*** (0.009)	0.024*** (0.004)	-0.021** (0.010)	0.015* (0.003
	.916*** 0.207)	0.881*** (0.225)	0.918*** (0.240)	0.142 (0.132)	1.006*** (0.299)	0.592*** (0.232)	1.011*** (0.252)	0.070 (0.114)	3.252*** (0.317)	0.998* (0.344
	.358	0.438	0.566	2.245	0.743	1.688	0.666	3.153	76.22	1.556
	.991	2635	2326	502	1824	1276	1142	508	14	768
	7314.43	-6545.73	-5929.82	-1463.46	-4386.66	-3781.54	-2313.02	-1488.53	-20.779	-2225.

adjusted over countries, in parentheses.
ercent (p < 0.01), **Significance at 5 percent (p < 0.05), *Significance at 10 percent p < 0.10 (two–tailed)
rship and women's political rights dropped because of collinearity with constant.

ative binomial regression of domestic terrorist attack counts on economic and political inde
s (1981-2002)

Model 1	Model 2 OECD	Model 3 Non OECD	Model 4 Democracy	Model 5 Dictatorship	Model 6 OECD/ Democracy	Model 7 OECD/ Dictatorship	Model 8 Non OECD/ Democracy
-0.072***	-0.076***	-0.055***	-0.084***	-0.056***	-0.068 ***	-0.480***	-0.061***
(0.011)	(0.016)	(0.013)	(0.015)	(.0017)	(0.017)	(0.143)	(0.020)
-0.159	0.078	-0.284*	-0.205	-0.206	0.047	9.224***	-0.325*
(0.161)	(0.327)	(0.159)	(0.206)	(0.214)	(0.313)	(2.442)	(0.190)
0.252	-0.351	0.210	0.217	0.267)	-0.388	omitted	0.276
(0.194)	(0.297)	(0.208)	0.186)	(0.323)	(0.289)		(0.198)
0.848**	-0.277	1.136**	0.805***	1.617**	-0.292	omitted	1.392**
(0.355)	(0.754)	(0.326)	(0.400)	(0.736)	(0.710)		(0.401)
2.32e-06*	0.00001**	1.57e-06**	2.02e-06	1.98e-06**	0.00001**	-0.0002**	-2.21e-06**
(1.22e-06)	(5.74e-06)	(7.39e-07)	(3.91e-06)	(8.13e-07)	(5.53e-06)	(0.00007)	(1.00e-06)
3.57e-06	-0.00003	-0.00001	0.00002	-0.00002	-.00004**	-0.008***	0.00002
(0.00001)	(0.00002)	(0.00002)	(0.00002)	(0.00002)	(0.00002)	(0.002)	(0.00004)
0.111**	-0.058	0.104**					
(0.043)	(0.235)	(0.045)					
0.022***	0.024***	0.019***	0.020***	0.032***	0.024***	-0.007***	0.016***
(0.005)	(0.006)	(0.004)	(0.004)	(0.010)	(0.006)	(0.001)	(0.003)
0.890***	-0.169	1.022***	0.488**	1.067***	-0.177	4.075***	1.042**
(0.260)	(0.143)	(0.325)	(0.255)	(0.291)	(0.114)	(0.967)	(0.365)
0.243	-0.169	0.376	1.372	0.346	2.963	84.797	1.156
2326	502	1824	1276	1142	508	14	768
-4873.22	-1156.96	-3639.92	-3145.38	-1840.13	-1171.05	-18.449	-1909.54

ors, adjusted over countries, in parentheses.
1 percent (p < 0.01), **Significance at 5 percent ($p < 0.05$), *Significance at 10 percent
adership and women's political rights dropped because of collinearity with constant.

binomial regression of transnational terrorist attack counts on economic and political
untries (1981-2002)

	Model 1	Model 2 OECD	Model 3 Non OECD	Model 4 Democracy	Model 5 Dictatorship	Model 6 OECD/ Democracy	Model 7 Non OECD/ Democracy	Model 8 Non OECD/ Dictatorship
	0.038*** (0.01)	-0.042** (0.019)	-0.025** (0.011)	-0.053*** (0.014)	-0.018 (0.013)	-0.041** (0.020)	-0.041*** (0.016)	-0.017 (0.013)
	0.067 (0.178)	0.522 (0.353)	-0.335** (0.124)	0.226 (0.227)	-0.319** (0.153)	0.551 (0.336)	-0.254 (0.182)	-0.414** (0.157)
	-0.054 (0.138)	-0.594** (0.267)	0.034 (0.138)	-0.187 (0.184)	0.100 (0.202)	-0.651** (0.270)	0.072 (0.180)	0.036 (0.189)
	0.326 (0.441)	-0.350 (0.910)	0.632 (0.458)	0.358 (0.456)	1.314* (0.794)	-0.433 (0.869)	0.745 (0.505)	1.256 (0.758)
	1.25e-06* (7.70e-07)	3.51e-06 (5.04e-06)	8.55e-07 (8.02e-07)	-3.87e-07 (1.81e-06)	1.26e-06*** (4.76e-07)	2.53e-06 (4.23e-06)	-2.85e-06* (1.59e-06)	1.14e-06*** (2.90e-07)
	0.00001 (0.00001)	-0.00004 (0.00003)	6.10e-06 (0.00001)	0.00003 (0.00002)	9.28e-06 (0.00002)	-0.00003 (0.00003)	0.00004 (0.00003)	2.65e-06 (0.00001)
	0.119*** (0.037)	0.064 (0.198)	0.116** (0.038)					
	0.014*** (0.003)	0.020*** (0.005)	0.010*** (0.002)	0.014*** (0.003)	0.015* (0.008)	0.020*** (0.004)	0.010*** (0.002)	0.011*** (0.003)
	0.750*** (0.244)	-0.144 (0.185)	0.898*** (0.302)	0.447* (0.263)	0.967*** (0.205)	-0.249 (0.163)	0.854*** (0.330)	1.006*** (0.210)
	0.821	1.171	-0.645	0.388	-0.655	1.728	0.288	-0.449
	2326	502	1824	1276	1142	508	768	1128
	3359.58	-897.73	-2397.851	-2242.22	-1225.13	-917.815	-1273.946	-1191.034

adjusted over countries, in parentheses.
rcent ($p < 0.01$), **Significance at 5 percent ($p < 0.05$), *Significance at 10 percent $p < 0.10$ (two-tailed)
CD countries with dictatorship did not converge.

References:

(DAW), United Nations. (2005). Impact of Women's Participation in Decision-making, Expert Group Meeting on Equal participation of women and men in decision-making processes, with particular emphasis on political participation and leadership *Report of the Expert Group Meeting*. Addis-Ababa, Ethiopia: Division for the Advancement of Women
Department of Economic and Social Affairs.

(IPU), Inter-Parliamentary Union. (2012). Women in National Parliaments. Retrieved October 2012 www.ipu.org\wmn-e\world.htm

(UNDP), United Nations Development Programme. (1995). Human Development Report. Oxford University Press: United Nations.

Abadie, Alberto. (2006). Poverty, Political Freedom, and the Roots of Terrorism. *The American Economic Review, 96*(2), 50-56.

Agarwal, Bina. (2010). Does Women's Proportional Strength Affect their Participation? Governing Local Forests in South Asia. *World Development, 38*(1), 98-112.

Akerkar, Supriya. (2001). Gender and participation. *BRIDGE Cutting Edge Pack, Brighton: Institute of Development Studies*.

Alexander, Deborah. , & Andersen, Kristi (1993). Gender as a Factor in the Attribution of Leadership Traits. *Political Research Quarterly, 46*(3), 527-545.

Alison, Miranda. (2003). Cogs in the Wheel? Women in the Liberation Tigers of Tamil Eelam. *Civil Wars, 6*(4), 37-54. doi: 10.1080/1369824042000221367

Alison, Miranda. (2004). Women as Agents of Political Violence: Gendering Security. *Security Dialogue, 35*(4), 447-463. doi: 10.1177/0967010604049522

Anderlini, Sanam Naraghi. (2000). Women at the peace table. New York: UN Development Fund for Women.

Asal, Victor, & Rethemeyer, R. Karl. (2006). Researching Terrorist Networks. *Journal of Security Education, 1*(4), 65-74. doi: 10.1300/J460v01n04_06

Asal, Victor, & Rethemeyer, R. Karl. (2008). The Nature of the Beast: Organizational Structures and the Lethality of Terrorist Attacks. *Journal of Politics, 70*(2), 437-449.

Atran, Scott, & Ginges, Jeremy. (2012). RELIGIOUS AND SACRED IMPERATIVES IN HUMAN CONFLICT. *Science, 336*(6083), 855-857. doi: 10.2307/41584849

Ballington, J. (2008). *Equality in Politics: A survey of Women and Men in Parliaments*: Inter-parliamentary union.

Beer, Caroline. (2009). Democracy and Gender Equality. *Studies in Comparative International Development, 44*(3), 212-227.

Belli, Roberta (2012). Financial Crime and Political Extremism in the U.S. University of Maryland.: The National Consortium for the Study of Terrorism and Responses to Terrorism (START)

Berko, Anat, & Erez, Edna. (2007). Gender, Palestinian Women, and Terrorism: Women's Liberation or Oppression? *Studies in Conflict & Terrorism, 30*(6), 493-519. doi: 10.1080/10576100701329550

Berman, Eli. (2009). *Radical, religious, and violent: the new economics of terrorism*: The MIT Press.

Bjarnegård, Elin, & Melander, Erik. (2011). Disentangling gender, peace and democratization: the negative effects of militarized masculinity. *Journal of Gender Studies, 20*(2), 139-154. doi: 10.1080/09589236.2011.565194

Blanchard, Eric M. (2003). Gender, International Relations, and the Development of Feminist Security Theory. *Signs, 28*(4), 1289-1312.

Bloom, Mia. (2005). *Dying to Kill.* New York: Columbia University Press.

Bloom, Mia. (2011). Bombshells: Women and Terror. *Gender Issues, 28*(1/2), 1-21. doi: 10.1007/s12147-011-9098-z

Braithwaite, Alex, & Li, Quan. (2007). Transnational Terrorism Hot Spots: Identification and Impact Evaluation. *Conflict Management and Peace Science, 24*(4), 281-296. doi: http://cmp.sagepub.com/archive/

Bravo, Ana Bela Santos, & Dias, Carlos Manuel Mendes (2006). An Empirical Analysis Of Terrorism: Deprivation, Islamism And Geopolitical Factors. *Defence & Peace Economics, 17*(4), 329-341. doi: 10.1080/10242690500526509

Brockhoff, Sarah, Krieger, Tim, & Meierrieks, Daniel. (2010). Ties That Do Not Bind (Directly): The Education-Terrorism Nexus Revisited. from CIE Center for International Economics

Burgoon, Brian. (2006). On Welfare and Terror: Social Welfare Policies and Political-Economic Roots of Terrorism. *The Journal of Conflict Resolution, 50*(2), 176-203.

Caiazza, Amy. (2001). Why gender matters in understanding September 11: Women, militarism, and violence *Publication no. 1908.* Washington, DC: Institute for Women's Policy Research.

Caprioli, Mary. (2000). Gendered Conflict. *Journal of Peace Research, 37*(1), 51-68.

Caprioli, Mary. (2003a). Gender Equality and Civil Wars: CPR Unit of the World Bank.

Caprioli, Mary. (2003b). Gender Equality and State Aggression: The Impact of Domestic Gender Equality on State First Use of Force. *International Interactions, 29*(3), 195.

Caprioli, Mary. (2004). Feminist IR Theory and Quantitative Methodology: A Critical Analysis. *International Studies Review, 6*(2), 253-269.

Caprioli, Mary. (2005). Primed for Violence: The Role of Gender Inequality in Predicting Internal Conflict. *International Studies Quarterly, 49*(2), 161-178.

Caprioli, Mary, & Boyer, Mark A. (2001). Gender, Violence, and International Crisis. *The Journal of Conflict Resolution, 45*(4), 503-518.

Caprioli, Mary, Emmett, Chad, Hudson, Valerie M., Spanvill, Bonnie Ballif-, & McDermott, Rose. (2007). Putting women in their place. *Baker Center Journal of Applied Public Policy, 1*(1), 12- 24.

Cheibub, José, Gandhi, Jennifer, & Vreeland, James. (2010). Democracy and dictatorship revisited. *Public Choice, 143*(1), 67-101. doi: 10.1007/s11127-009-9491-2

Chen, D. (2004). Gender equality and economic development: the role for information and communication technologies. *World Bank Policy Research Working Paper*(3285).

Choi, Seung-Whan. (2010). Fighting Terrorism through the Rule of Law? *Journal of Conflict Resolution, 54*(6), 940-966. doi: 10.1177/0022002710371666

Cingranelli, David L., & Richards, David L. (2010). The Cingranelli and Richards (CIRI) Human Rights Data Project. *Human Rights Quarterly, 32*(2), 401-424.

Cockburn, C. (1999). *The space between us: Negotiating gender and national identities in conflict*: Zed books.

Cockburn, C. (2001). The gendered dynamics of armed conflict and political violence. In C. Moser & F. C. Clark (Eds.), *Victims, perpetrators or actors* (pp. 13-29). London: Zed.

Cook, David. (2005). Women Fighting in Jihad ? *Studies in Conflict & Terrorism, 28*(5), 375-384. doi: 10.1080/10576100500180212

Cooper, H.H. A. . (1979). Women as Terrorist. In F. Adler & R. J. Simon (Eds.), *The Criminology of Deviant Women*. Boston: Houghton Mifflin.

Crenshaw, Martha. (1981). The Causes of Terrorism. *Comparative Politics, 13*(4), 379-399.

Crenshaw, Martha. (1989). *Terrorism and International Cooperation*: Institute for East-West Security Studies New York, NY.

Crenshaw, Martha. (2010). Thoughts on Relating Terrorism to Historical Contexts. In M. Crenshaw (Ed.), *Terrorism in Context*: Pennsylvania State University Press.

Cunningham, Karla J. (2003). Cross-Regional Trends in Female Terrorism. *Studies in Conflict & Terrorism, 26*(3), 171-195. doi: 10.1080/10576100390211419

Dalton, Angela, & Asal, Victor. (2011). Is It Ideology or Desperation: Why Do Organizations Deploy Women in Violent Terrorist Attacks? *Studies in Conflict & Terrorism, 34*(10), 802-819. doi: 10.1080/1057610x.2011.604833

Detraz, Nicole. (2012). *International security and gender*. Cambridge, UK: Malden, MA.

Dreher, A., & Fischer, J.A.V. (2011). Does government decentralization reduce domestic terror? An empirical test. *Economics Letters, 111*(3), 223-225.

Elshtain, Jean Bethke. (1987). *Women and war*. New York: Basic Books.

Enders, Walter, & Sandler, Todd. (2000). Is Transnational Terrorism Becoming More Threatening? A Time-Series Investigation. *The Journal of Conflict Resolution, 44*(3), 307-332.

Enders, Walter, & Sandler, Todd. (2002). Patterns of Transnational Terrorism, 1970-1999: Alternative Time-Series Estimates. *International Studies Quarterly, 46*(2), 145-165.

Enders, Walter, Sandler, Todd, & Gaibulloev, Khusrav. (2011). Domestic versus transnational terrorism: Data, decomposition, and dynamics. *Journal of Peace Research, 48*(3), 319-337. doi: 10.1177/0022343311398926

Enloe, Cynthia. (1983). *Does Khaki Become You? The Militarization of Women's Lives*. London: Pluto Press.

Enloe, Cynthia. (1990). *Bananas, Beaches and Bases: Making Feminist Sense of International Politics*. Berkeley: University of California Press.

Enloe, Cynthia. (2007). *Globalization and Militarism; Feminists Make the Link*: Rowman & Littlefield Publishers, Inc.

Eubank, William, & Weinberg, Leonard. (1994). Does democracy encourage terrorism? *Terrorism and Political Violence, 6*(4), 417-435.

Eubank, William, & Weinberg, Leonard. (2001). Terrorism and Democracy: Perpetrators and Victims. *Terrorism and Political Violence, 13*(1), 155-164. doi: 10.1080/09546550109609674

Eyerman, Joe. (1998). Terrorism and democratic states: Soft targets or accessible systems. *International Interactions, 24*(2), 151-170. doi: 10.1080/03050629808434924

Feldmann, Andreas E., & Perälä, Maiju. (2004). Reassessing the Causes of Nongovernmental Terrorism in Latin America. *Latin American Politics and Society, 46*(2), 101-132.

Fox, Jonathan. (2004). The Rise of Religious Nationalism and Conflict: Ethnic Conflict and Revolutionary Wars, 1945-2001. *Journal of Peace Research, 41*(6), 715-731. doi: 10.2307/4149714

Fox, Jonathan, & Sandler, Shmuel. (2004). *Bringing religion into international relations*: Cambridge Univ Press.

Freytag, Andreas, Krüger, Jens J., Meierrieks, Daniel, & Schneider, Friedrich. (2011). The origins of terrorism: Cross-country estimates of socio-economic determinants of terrorism. *European Journal of Political Economy, 27, Supplement 1*(0), S5-S16.

Friedman, Marilyn. (2008). Female Terrorists: What Difference Does Gender Make? *Social Philosophy Today, 23*, 189-200.

Galvin, Deborah M. (1983). The Female Terrorist: A Socio-Psychological Perspective. *Behavioral Sciences & the Law, 1*(2), 19-32.

Gassebner, Martin., & Luechinger, Simon. (2011). Lock, stock, and barrel: A comprehensive assessment of the determinants of terror. *Public Choice, 149*(3), 235-261.

Gause III, F. Gregory. (2005). Can Democracy Stop Terrorism? *Foreign Affairs, 84*(5), 62-76.

Gentry, Caron E, & Sjoberg, Laura. (2011). The Gendering of Women's Terrorism. In L. Sjoberg & C. E. Gentry (Eds.), *Women, Gender, and Terrorism*. Athens and London: The University of Georgia Press.

Gentry, Caron E. (2009). Twisted Maternalism. *International Feminist Journal of Politics, 11*(2), 235-252. doi: 10.1080/14616740902789609

Giles, Wenona, & Hyndman, Jennifer (Eds.). (2004). *Sites of Violence: Gender and Conflict Zones*. Berkeley: University of California Press. .

Gilligan, Carol. (1982). *In a different voice : psychological theory and women's development*. Cambridge, Mass.: Harvard University Press.

Gleditsch, Nils Petter, Wallensteen, Peter, Eriksson, Mikael, Sollenberg, Margareta, & Strand, Havard. (2002). Armed Conflict 1946-2001: A New Dataset. *Journal of Peace Research, 39*(5), 615.

Goldstein, J.S. (2003). *War and gender: How gender shapes the war system and vice versa*: Cambridge University Press.

Gunawardena, Arjuna. (2006). Female black tigers: A different breed of cat? *Female suicide bombers: Dying for equality*, 81-90.

Hawkesworth, Mary. (2008). War as Mode of Production and Reproduction: Femninist Analytics. In K. Alexander & M. Hawkesworth (Eds.), *War & terror: feminist perspectives*: University of Chicago Press Journals.

Heston, Alan, Summers, Robert , & Aten, Bettina (2009). Penn World Table Version 6.3. from Center for International Comparisons of Production, Income and Prices at the University of Pennsylvania.

Hoffman, Bruce. (1995). "Holy terror": The Implications of Terrorism Motivated by a Religious Imperative. *Studies in Conflict & Terrorism, 18*(4), 271-284.

Hoffman, Bruce. (1999). *Inside Terrorism*. New York: Columbia University Press.

Hoffman, Bruce. (2006). *Inside Terrorism* (Second ed.). New York: Columbia University Press.

Hoffman, Bruce, & McCormick, Gordon H. (2004). Terrorism, Signaling, and Suicide Attack. *Studies in Conflict & Terrorism, 27*(4), 243-281.

Höglund, Anna T. (2003). War on terrorism: Feminist and ethical perspectives. *Security Dialogue, 34*(2), 242.

Htun, Mala. (2003). *Sex and the State: Abortion, Divorce, and the Family under Latin American Dictatorships and Democracies*: Cambridge University Press

Huber, Wolfgang. (2011). Religion and violence in a globalised world. *Verbum et Ecclesia, 32*(2), 39-46. doi: 10.4102/ve.v32i2.581

Hudson, Valerie M. (2012). *Sex and world peace*. New York: Columbia University Press.

Hudson, Valerie M., Caprioli, Mary, Ballif-Spanvill, Bonnie, McDermott, Rose, & Emmett, Chad F. (2008). The Heart of the Matter: The Security of Women and the Security of States. *International Security, 33*(3), 7-45.

Hunt, Krista , & Rygiel, Kim (Eds.). (2006). *(En)Gendering the War on Terror: War Stories and Camouflaged Politics Gender in a Global/ Local World*: Ashgate.

Iannaccone, Laurence R., & Berman, Eli. (2006). Religious extremism: The good, the bad, and the deadly. *Public Choice, 128*(1/2), 109-129. doi: 10.1007/s11127-006-9047-7

Ii, William F. Shughart. (2006). An Analytical History of Terrorism, 1945-2000. *Public Choice, 128*(1/2), 7-39.

Inglehart, Ronald, & Norris, Pippa. (2003). *Rising Tide: Gender Equality and Cultural Change Around the World*. Cambridge, UK. New York, USA.: Cambridge University Press.

Jacques, Karen, & Taylor, Paul J. (2009). Female Terrorism: A Review. *Terrorism and Political Violence, 21*(3), 499-515. doi: 10.1080/09546550902984042

Jenkins, Brian Michael. (1980). The study of Terrorism: Definitional problems *The Rand paper series*. Santa Monica, California: RAND.

Johnson, Allan G. (2010). Patriarchy. In P. S. Rothenberg (Ed.), *Race, Class and Gender in the United States* (Eighth ed., pp. 153- 161). New York: Worth Publishers.

Juergensmeyer, Mark. (2001). Terror in the Name of God. *Current History, 100*(649), 357-361.

Juergensmeyer, Mark. (2003). *Terror in the mind of God : the global rise of religious violence* (Third ed.). Berkley and Los Angeles: University of California Press.

Kabeer, Naila. (1999a). From Feminist Insights to an Analytical Framework: An Institutional Perspective on Gender Inequality In N. Kabeer & R. Subrahmanian

(Eds.), *Institutions, Relations and Outcomes: Framework and Case Studies for Gender- Aware Planning*. (pp. 435). London: ZedPub.

Kabeer, Naila. (1999b). Resources, agency, achievements: Reflections on the measurement of women's empowerment. *Development and change, 30*(3), 435-464.

Kabeer, Naila. (2005). Gender equality and women's empowerment: A critical analysis of the third millennium development goal 1. *Gender & Development, 13*(1), 13-24. doi: 10.1080/13552070512331332273

Karl, Marilee. (1995). *Women and Empowerment: Participation and Decision Making* London and New Jersey: Zed Books.

Kaufman, Joyce P., & Williams, Kristen P. (2007). *Women, the state, and war: a comparative perspective on citizenship and nationalism.* Lanham, MD, USA and Plymouth UK: Lexington Books.

Kis-Katos, Krisztina, Liebert, Helge, & Schulze, Günther G. (2011). On the origin of domestic and international terrorism. *European Journal of Political Economy, 27*, S17-S36.

Koch, M.T., & Fulton, S.A. (2011). In the defense of women: Gender, office holding, and national security policy in established democracies. *The Journal of Politics, 73*(01), 1-16.

Krieger, Tim, & Meierrieks, Daniel. (2010). Terrorism in the worlds of welfare capitalism. *Journal of Conflict Resolution, 54*(6), 902-939.

Krieger, Tim, & Meierrieks, Daniel. (2011). What causes terrorism? *Public Choice, 147*(1), 3-27. doi: 10.1007/s11127-010-9601-1

Krueger, Alan B. (2008). *What makes a terrorist: economics and the roots of terrorism (New Edition)*: Princeton University Press.

Kunz, Rahel, & Sjoberg, Ann-Kristin. (2009). Empowered or Oppressed? Female Combatants in the Colombian Guerrilla: The Case of the Revolutionary Armed Forced of Colombia - FARC. *Conference Papers -- International Studies Association*, 1-33.

Kydd, Andrew H., & Walter, Barbara F. (2006). The Strategies of Terrorism. *International Security, 31*(1), 49-80.

LaFree, Gary, & Dugan, Laura. (2007). Introducing the Global Terrorism Database. *Terrorism & Political Violence, 19*(2), 181-204. doi: 10.1080/09546550701246817

Lai, Brian. (2007a). 'Draining the Swamp': An Empirical Examination of the Production of International Terrorism, 1968-1998. *Conflict Management and Peace Science, 24*(4), 297-310. doi: http://cmp.sagepub.com/archive/

Lai, Brian. (2007b). "Draining the Swamp": Examination of the Production of International Terrorism, 1968—1998 *Conflict Management and Peace Science, 24*(4), 297-310. doi: 10.1080/07388940701643649

Li, Quan. (2005). Does Democracy Promote or Reduce Transnational Terrorist Incidents? *The Journal of Conflict Resolution, 49*(2), 278-297.

Li, Quan, & Schaub, Drew. (2004). Economic Globalization and Transnational Terrorism: A Pooled Time-Series Analysis. *The Journal of Conflict Resolution, 48*(2), 230-258.

Long, J. Scott, & Freese, Jeremy (2006). *Regression Models for Categorical Dependent Variables Using Stata* (second ed.). College Station TX: Stata Press.

Marshall, M. G. , & Jaggers, K. . (2002). Polity IV Project: Political Regime Characteristics and Transitions, 1800-2002: Dataset Users' Manual. from University of Maryland.

Mazurana, Dyan E. , Raven-Roberts, Angela, & Parpart, Jane L. (2005). *Gender, conflict, and peacekeeping*: Rowman & Littlefield.

McCormick, Gordon H. (2003). TERRORIST DECISION MAKING. *Annual Review of Political Science, 6*(1), 473-507.

Melander, Erik. (2005). Gender Equality and Intrastate Armed Conflict. *International Studies Quarterly, 49*(4), 695-714.

Mickolus, Edward F. (1984). International Terrorism: Attributes of Terrorist Events, 1968-1977 [ITERATE 2]: Inter-university Consortium for Political and Social Research (ICPSR) [distributor]. Retrieved from http://dx.doi.org/10.3886/ICPSR07947.v1

Midlarsky, Manus I., Crenshaw, Martha, & Yoshida, Fumihiko. (1980). Why Violence Spreads: The Contagion of International Terrorism. *International Studies Quarterly, 24*(2), 262-298.

Miranda, Rosa Linda T (2005). *Impact of Women's Participation in Decision-making, Expert Group Meeting on Equal participation of women and men in decision-making processes, with particular emphasis on political participation and leadership* United Nations.

Mohanty, Chandra. . (2003). "Under western eyes" revisited: feminist solidarity through anticapitalist struggles. *Signs, 28*(2), 499-535.

Mohanty, Chandra. , Pratt, Minnie B., & Riley, Robin L. . (2008). Introduction: feminism and US wars-mapping the ground In C. M. Robin L. Riley, and Minnie B. Pratt. (Ed.), *Feminism and War: Confronting U.S. Imperialism*. London and New York: Zed Press. .

Moser, Caroline N. O. (2001). The Gendered Continuum of Violence and Conflict: an Operational Framework. In C. N. O. Moser & F. Clark (Eds.), *Victims, Perpetrators or Actors?: Gender, Armed Conflict and Political Violence*: Zed Press.

Nacos, Brigitte L. (2005). The Portrayal of Female Terrorists in the Media: Similar Framing Patterns in the News Coverage of Women in Politics and in Terrorism. *Studies in Conflict & Terrorism, 28*(5), 435-451. doi: 10.1080/10576100500180352

Ness, Cindy D. (2005). In the Name of the Cause: Women's Work in Secular and Religious Terrorism. *Studies in Conflict & Terrorism, 28*(5), 353-373. doi: 10.1080/10576100500180337

Newman, Edward. (2006). Exploring the "root causes" of terrorism. *Studies in Conflict & Terrorism, 29*(8), 749-772.

O'Rourke, Lindsey A. (2009). What's Special about Female Suicide Terrorism? *Security Studies, 18*(4), 681-718. doi: 10.1080/09636410903369084

Obama, Barak (2010). *The National Security Strategy* Washington DC.

Oberschall, Anthony. (2004). Explaining terrorism: The contribution of collective action theory. *Sociological Theory, 22*(1), 26-37.

Pankhurst, D. (2009). Sexual Violence in War. *Gender Matters in Global Politics: A Feminist Introduction to International Relations*. London: Routledge, 148-160.

Pape, Robert. (2003). The Strategic Logic of Suicide Terrorism. *The American Political Science Review, 97*(3), 343-361.

Parashar, Swati. (2011). Gender, Jihad, and Jingoism : Women as Perpetrators, Planners, and Patrons of Militancy in Kashmir. *Studies in Conflict & Terrorism, 34*(4), 295-317. doi: 10.1080/1057610x.2011.551719

Pfau-Effinger, Birgit. (1998). Gender Cultures and the Gender Arrangement -- A Theoretical Framework for Cross-National Gender Research. *Innovation: The European Journal of Social Sciences, 11*(2), 147-166.

Piazza, James A. (2006). Rooted in Poverty?: Terrorism, Poor Economic Development, and Social Cleavages 1. *Terrorism & Political Violence, 18*(1), 159-177. doi: 10.1080/095465590944578

Piazza, James A. (2008). Incubators of Terror: Do Failed and Failing States Promote Transnational Terrorism? *International Studies Quarterly, 52*(3), 469-488.

Piazza, James A. (2011). Poverty, minority economic discrimination, and domestic terrorism. *Journal of Peace Research, 48*(3), 339-353. doi: 10.1177/0022343310397404

Pillar, Paul R. (2001). *Terrorism and U.S. foreign policy*: Brookings Institution Press.

Plümper, Thomas, & Neumayer, Eric. (2006). The Unequal Burden of War: The Effect of Armed Conflict on the Gender Gap in Life Expectancy. *International Organization, 60*(3), 723-754.

Ranstorp, Magnus. (1996). Terrorism in the Name of Religion. *JOURNAL OF INTERNATIONAL AFFAIRS-COLUMBIA UNIVERSITY, 50*, 41-62.

Regan, Patrick M., & Paskeviciute, Aida. (2003). Women's Access to Politics and Peaceful States. *Journal of Peace Research, 40*(3), 287.

Robison, Kristopher K. (2010). Unpacking the Social Origins of Terrorism: The Role of Women's Empowerment in Reducing Terrorism. *Studies in Conflict & Terrorism, 33*(8), 735-756. doi: 10.1080/1057610x.2010.494171

Robison, Kristopher K., Crenshaw, Edward M., & Jenkins, J. Craig. (2006). Ideologies of Violence: The Social Origins of Islamist and Leftist Transnational Terrorism. *Social Forces, 84*(4), 2009-2026.

Rogers, W. (1994). Regression standard errors in clustered samples. *Stata technical bulletin, 3*(13).

Ross, Jeffrey Ian. (1993). Structural causes of oppositional political terrorism: Towards a causal model. *Journal of Peace Research, 30*(3), 317.

Runyan, Anne Sisson, & Peterson, V. Spike (1991). The Radical Future of Realism: Feminist Subversions of IR Theory. *Alternatives: Global, Local, Political, 16*(1), 67-106.

Sánchez-Cuenca, Ignacio, & de la Calle, Luis. (2009). Domestic Terrorism: The Hidden Side of Political Violence. *Annual Review of Political Science, 12*(1), 31-49.

Sandler, Todd. (2003). Collective action and transnational terrorism. *The World Economy, 26*(6), 779-802.

Sandler, Todd. , & Lapan, Harvey E. . (1988). The Calculus of Dissent: An Analysis of Terrorist' Choice of Target. *Synthese, 76*, 245-261.

Satana, Nil S, Inman, Molly, & Birnir, Jóhanna Kristín. (2013). Religion, Government Coalitions, and Terrorism. *Terrorism and Political Violence, 25*(1), 29-52.

Schmid, Alex. (1992). The response problem as a definition problem. *Terrorism and Political Violence, 4*(4), 7-13. doi: 10.1080/09546559208427172

Schmid, Alex, & Jongman, Albert. (1988). *Political Terrorism*. New Brunswick, NJ: Transaction.

Schweitzer, Yoram. (2006). *Female suicide bombers: dying for equality?* : Jaffee Center for Strategic Studies, Tel Aviv University.

Sjoberg, Laura. (2009). Introduction to Security Studies: Feminist Contributions. *Security Studies, 18*(2), 183-213. doi: 10.1080/09636410902900129

Sjoberg, Laura. (2010). Introduction. In L. Sjoberg (Ed.), *Gender and international security : feminist perspectives*. London, UK, New York Routledge.

Sjoberg, Laura, Cooke, Grace D., & Neal, Stacy R. (2011). Introduction: Women, Gender, and Terrorism In L. Sjoberg & C. E. Gentry (Eds.), *Women, Gender, and Terorism*. Athens and London: The University of Georgia Press.

Sjoberg, Laura, & Gentry, Caron E. (2007). *Mothers, monsters, whores : women's violence in global politics*

Speckhard, Anne. (2008). The Emergence of Female Suicide Terrorists. *Studies in Conflict & Terrorism, 31*(11), 1023-1051. doi: 10.1080/10576100802408121

Spivak, G.C. (1988). Can the subaltern speak?

Stack, Alisa. (2011). Zombies versus Black Widows. In L. Sjoberg & C. E. Gentry (Eds.), *Women, Gender, and Terrorism*. Athens and London: The University of Georgia Press.

Steans, Jill. (2003). Engaging from the margins: feminist encounters with the with the 'mainstream' of International Relations. *British Journal of Politics & International Relations, 5*(3), 428-454. doi: 10.1111/1467-856x.00114

Sutton, Barbara, & Novkov, Julie. (2008). Rethinking Security, Confronting Inequality. In B. Sutton, S. Morgen & J. Novkov (Eds.), *Security Disarmed: Critical Perspectives on Gender, Race, and Militarization*. . New Brunswick, NJ: Rutgers University Press.

Sykes, Patricia Lee. (1993). Women as national leaders: Patterns and prospects. *SAGE FOCUS EDITIONS, 153*, 219-219.

Teorell, Jan, Nicholas Charron, Marcus Samanni, Sören Holmberg & Bo Rothstein. (2011). The Quality of Government Dataset. Retrieved January 12, 2012, from University of Gothenburg: The Quality of Government Institute http://www.qog.pol.gu.se

Thobani, Sunera. (2007). White wars: Western feminisms and the `War on Terror'. *Feminist Theory, 8*(2), 169-185. doi: 10.1177/1464700107078140

Tickner, J. Ann. (1992). *Gender in international relations : feminist perspectives on achieving global security* New York Columbia University Press.

Tickner, J. Ann. (1997). You Just Don't Understand: Troubled Engagements between Feminists and IR Theorists. *International Studies Quarterly, 41*(4), 611-632.

Tickner, J. Ann. (2001). *Gendering World Politics* New York: Columbia University Press.
Towns, Anne E. . (2010). *Women and States- norms and hierarchies in international society*. New York: Cambridge University Press.
Tremblay, Manon. (2007). Democracy, Representation, and Women: A Comparative Analysis. *Democratization, 14*(4), 533-553. doi: 10.1080/13510340701398261
UN. (2000). *Resolution 1325* (S/RES/1325 (2000)). New York: United Nations Retrieved from http://www.un.org/events/res_1325e.pdf.
UN. (2004). *Women and peace and security: Report of the Secretary-General*. New York, NY: United Nations.
Urdal, Henrik. (2006). A clash of generations? Youth bulges and political violence. *International Studies Quarterly, 50*(3), 607-629.
Von Knop, Katharina. (2007). The Female Jihad: Al Qaeda's Women. *Studies in Conflict & Terrorism, 30*(5), 397-414. doi: 10.1080/10576100701258585
Wade, Sara Jackson. , & Reiter, Dan. (2007). Does Democracy Matter? Regime Type and Suicide Terrorism. *The Journal of Conflict Resolution, 51*(2), 329-348.
Walsh, Denise (2011). *Women's Rights in Democratizing States: Just Debate and Gender Justice in the Public Sphere*. New York: Cambridge University Press.
Walsh, J.I., & Piazza, J.A. (2010). Why respecting physical integrity rights reduces terrorism. *Comparative Political Studies, 43*(5), 551-577.
WDR. (2012). World Development Report: Gender Equality and Development Washington D.C.: The World bank.
Weinberg, Leonard, & Eubank, William. (2011). Women's Involvement in Terrorism. *Gender Issues, 28*(1/2), 22-49. doi: 10.1007/s12147-011-9101-8
West, Candace, & Don, H. Zimmerman. (1987). Doing Gender. *Gender and Society, 1*(2), 125-151.
WfWi. (2008). 2008 Iraq Report: Amplifying the Voices of Women in Iraq *Stronger Women Stronger Nations*: Women for Women International.
WfWi. (2009). 2009 Afghanistan Report: Amplifying the Voices of Women in Afghanistan: Women for Women International.
WfWi. (2010). 2010 DRC Report: Amplifying the Voices of Women in Eastern Congo *Stronger Women Stronger Nations*: Women for Women International.
White, Jonathan R. . (2012). *Terrorism and Homeland Security* (7th ed.): Wadsworth, Cengage Learning
Wilkinson, Paul. (2011). *Terrorism versus democracy : the liberal state response* (3rd ed.). Abingdon, Oxon: New York.
Williams, R.L. (2000). A note on robust variance estimation for cluster,Äêcorrelated data. *Biometrics, 56*(2), 645-646.
World Values Survey (2000). from World Values Survey Association
Zalewski, M. . (1993). Feminist Standpoint Meets International Relations Theory: A Feminist Version of David and Goliath. *The Fletcher Forum of World Affairs, 17*(2), 221-229.

Chapter 3: Actions speak louder than words: Measuring the Impact of Gender Equality Attitudes and Outcomes as Deterrents of Terrorism

3.1 Introduction

Recent research suggests that level of gender equality[1] in a country is a predictor of whether a country will experience internal conflict, political violence and terrorism. There is growing recognition that terrorism is a political act with social roots. These social interactions emerge out of the cultural attitudes, beliefs and norms of the societies in which terrorists operate. Studies show that culture plays an integral role in shaping public attitudes towards gender equality (Inglehart & Norris, 2003; Norris & Inglehart, 2001). Scholars also emphasize the role of domestic culture in predicting political violence and intrastate conflict (Fox, 2001b; Gurr, 1994; Henderson, 1997; Mazrui, 1990). However, no study has empirically tested the impact of cultural attitudes on terrorism generally, and gender equality attitudes specifically, across a large number of countries over a relatively long period of time to analyze how much cultural attitudes matter and the direction of this relationship.

---

[1] This paper conceptualizes gender equality as the provision of equal opportunities to both men and women to develop their personal abilities. Gender equality does not imply sameness of sexes but envisions the presence and access to rights and opportunities for all individuals regardless of their sex. In practice, different societies differ in the social and cultural interpretation of biological differences between men and women and consequent distribution of responsibilities and resources leading to varying patterns of cross national gender inequalities.

This study is a cross-national times-series estimation for 57 countries for the period 1994-2002 that examines the impact of both cultural attitudes and actual outcomes of gender equality on levels of terrorism experienced by a country using World Values Survey (WVS) and Global Terrorism Database (GTD). The results suggest that actual outcomes of gender equality have a significant and consistently negative impact on both domestic and transnational terrorism. Women's actual advancement and equality in higher education, jobs and political representation are more effective in reducing terrorism than cultural attitudes that simply support these rights.

Furthermore, by comparing attitudes and actual outcomes of gender equality this paper identifies a gap between individual cultural attitudes towards gender equality and the collective institutional practices measured by actual progress towards achieving women's rights. These findings suggest a need to revisit policy perspectives that ignore the gap between cultural attitudes and actual practices. This study has important public policy implications for focusing on greater levels of social, economic and political gender equality for reducing levels of terrorism.

Cultural attitudes reflect peoples' beliefs and values and the actual outcomes are the result of the connections between culture and the overarching systems and structures. Cultural attitudes are gauged by public opinion, and to examine gender inequality attitudes this study focuses on three World Values Survey questions about women's right to education, work and political participation. This study conceptualizes gender equality outcomes as a synthesis of presence of effective gender equality policies (i.e. institutional set up), actual progress made with regard to women's rights (i.e. access to rights), and agency to avail that opportunity.

From a policy perspective this paper is concerned with looking at deterrents of terrorism. Overall both gender equality attitudes and actual outcomes matter, but only actual rights have a consistently negative impact on terrorism, which means that greater level of women's rights is associated with fewer terrorist attacks. The practice of women's rights seems to act as deterrent to terrorism because it tends to curtail and reverse the conditions that breed terrorism. Access to power and resources is critical for a just society, and gender inequality is a strong indicator of power asymmetry between men and women. The results suggest a causal explanation: as women are provided equal opportunities the society becomes more just and inclusive. This environment facilitates peaceful resolution of grievances through democratic and non-violent means, thus reducing the feelings of alienation, hopelessness and desperation that motivate terrorist acts. The central theoretical argument of this paper is that higher gender inequality in a country is an indication of social injustice, which in turn motivates terrorist activities.

The first section of this paper theorizes the links between increased gender equality and reduction in terrorism in a society. The second section empirically tests for the impact of cultural attitudes and outcomes of gender equality on overall terrorism, and also on domestic and transnational terrorism separately. The last section concludes with a discussion of the findings and their policy implications.

3.2 Literature Review

Terrorism is generally understood as a form of political action rooted in political and social discontent that legitimizes violence (Crenshaw, 1981). Some of the suggested predictors of terrorism include economic inequalities, political exclusion, political freedom, level of democracy, higher population growth especially in developing counties, a youth-age bulge, and socio-cultural factors (Abadie, 2006; Bravo & Dias, 2006; Dhillon, 2008; Eubank & Weinberg, 2001; Krieger & Meierrieks, 2011; Lai, 2007a; Li, 2005; Pape, 2003; Piazza, 2006, 2011; Urdal, 2006). There is growing consensus that terrorism is not just a political act but also a social phenomenon: a product of the social processes and relationship between states and their citizens (Crenshaw, 1981; Newman, 2006; Robison, 2010; Robison et al., 2006). Linked to the social dimension of terrorism, gender equality is an unconventional predictor of terrorism, which provides a deeper understanding of the gendered nature of violence and provides a stronger explanatory model of terrorism compared to conventional models.

Current research suggests a relationship exists between terrorism and domestic gender inequality. There is empirical evidence that female labor force participation influences terrorism (Berrebi & Ostwald, 2013; Robison, 2010; Robison et al., 2006). Broad literature on political violence suggests that higher domestic gender equality in a state is related to less internal conflict and more peaceful interstate relations (Caprioli, 2000, 2003b, 2005; Caprioli & Boyer, 2001; Melander, 2005; Regan & Paskeviciute, 2003). Caprioli (2005) argues that gender inequality is a robust measure of how tolerant a society is, and whether it is based on norms of equality. Even though women's equality is not the only predictor of violence, it is a consistent predictor of both internal conflict and international violence (Caprioli et al., 2007). Bjarnegård and Melander (2011) argue that democratic societies are peaceful only if there are effective moves toward attaining gender equality. Many national and international organizations advocate for improving the status of women to dissipate the factors which trigger political violence including terrorism (Anderlini, 2000; Farr, 2002; UN, 2004; WfWi, 2008, 2009, 2010). There is evidence that more robust women's rights in a society dispel the conditions associated with terrorism, for instance increases in women's rights and empowerment are associated with higher economic growth, improvement in quality of democracy and lower fertility rates ((WB), 1995, 2001; Beer, 2009; Kabeer, Stark, & Magnus, 2008; WDR, 2012).

Inglehart and Norris (2003) provide evidence that cultural attitudes towards gender equality explain the changes in socio-economic and political conditions in a country. Studies show that gender differences exist in cultural attitudes and social and political preferences (Atkeson & Rapoport, 2003; Croson & Gneezy, 2009). Women endorse socially compassionate policies more often than men (Eagly & Diekman, 2006), are more supportive of equal rights and social justice (Eagly, Diekman, Johannesen-schmidt, & Koenig, 2004; Nincic & Nincic, 2002), are less belligerent than men in almost all spheres of foreign and domestic policy (Page & Shapiro, 1992), are less supportive of defense spending (Eichenberg & Stoll, 2012) and are less likely to support use of force (deBoer, 1985; Fite, Genest, & Wilcox, 1990a; Smith, 1984; Togeby, 1994). Studying individual-level attitudes toward religiously motivated terrorism in Pakistan, Kaltenthaler, Miller, Ceccoli, and Gelleny (2010) found that men are more supportive of terrorism than women. An analysis of gender inequality attitudes and terrorism requires an understanding of the connections between culture and terrorism.

3.2.1 Terrorism and Culture

Terrorism and culture are linked in intricate ways. There is some literature that looks at how public attitudes are linked to political violence and terrorism (Anderson,

2011; Fite, Genest, & Wilcox, 1990b; Gadarian, 2010; Hetherington & Suhay, 2011; Kaltenthaler et al., 2010; Tessler & Warriner, 1997; Wiedenhaefer, Dastoor, Balloun, & Sosa-Fey, 2007). But so far there is no cross-national empirical study that tests the impact of cultural attitudes generally, and gender equality attitudes specifically, on terror attacks.

Scholars attribute higher levels of terrorism to certain demographic and cultural factors where aggression and violence are the preferred means of conflict resolution. Social behaviors, myths, habits and historical traditions that condone, sanction and justify use of violence, facilitate development of terrorism as a political norm (Anderson, 2011; Crenshaw, 1981; Gurr, 1990; Juergensmeyer, 2003). Culture is important to studying terrorism because it links collective identities to political action. For instance cultural identity plays a profound role as a mobilizing force in extremist groups like the Irish Republican Army (IRA), Palestine Liberation Organization (PLO) and the Liberation Tigers of Tamil Eelam (LTTE). Terrorism often arises out of a culture of alienation and grievance which sanctifies radicalization and extremism (Juergensmeyer, 2003; Newman, 2006; Stern, 2009). Grievance does not always lead to violence, and Caprioli (2005) emphasizes the need to examine the cultural norms that support violence as a legitimate means to address grievances. She suggests that such conditions are inherent to structural inequalities that lead to structural violence.

For the purpose of this essay culture is understood as a system of shared meaning and identity that people employ to manage daily life. It is the basis of social and political identity that influences behavior, choices, actions and priorities[2] (Laitin, 1986; M. H. Ross, 1997). Lichbach (1997) distinguishes between subjective and intersubjective views of culture. Subjective is how individuals internalize individual values and attitudes, while the intersubjective is the shared meaning and identities that constitute the symbolic and interpretative part of social life. This link suggests that there is a gap between the subjective / individual and intersubjective / institutional views of culture and the shared meaning. The 'subjective and intersubjective' framework can be employed to make a useful distinction between gender equality cultural attitudes and culturally constituted institutions and practices, and makes it feasible to test the hypotheses that there is a difference between gender equality attitudes and the institutional rights available to women reflected in the actual outcomes of those rights.

But why is it important to examine gender equality and terrorism? The answer lies in the gendered nature and consequences of political violence. The following section briefly describes the theoretical understandings of gender equality and political violence.

3.2.2 Connection between Gender Equality and Terrorism

The theoretical underpinnings for the connection between gender equality and terrorism are usually based on simplistic explanations that women are more averse to use of violence. This reasoning seems to be supported by evidence from criminology statistics where more than 90% of the homicide offenders are male, at least in the US[3].

---

[2] Geertz's defines culture ' as historically transmitted pattern of meaning embodied in symbols, a system of inherited conceptions expressed in symbolic forms by means of which men communicate, perpetuate, and develop their knowledge about, and attitudes towards life (1973b: 89).

[3] Federal Bureau of Investigation homicide data available at http://www.fbi.gov/about-us/cjis/ucr/crime-in-the-u.s/2010/crime-in-the-u.s.-2010/offenses-known-to-law-enforcement/expanded/expandhomicidemain

Sociological discourse on the construction of gender provides useful insights on the general perception that women are less likely to support violence than men. These feminist-pacifist propositions are based on association of women's experience of motherhood and their role as primary caregivers (Dietz, 1985; Elshtain, 1985; Ruddick, 1989). Socialization in a patriarchal society produces and reinforces gendered roles where reproductive labor of procreating, caring and nurturing is associated with women and femininity; and power, dominance and aggression with men and masculinity[4] (also see Johnson 1997).

Traditionally war and political violence have been men's domain and women are usually seen in supporting logistics roles (Eager, 2008; Goldstein, 2003). However this straightforward association of women and peace is doubtful given the long history of female terrorists, which debunks the myth that women are inherently or biologically more pacifistic than men. In fact women offer an obvious strategic advantage to terror groups as they arouse less suspicion due to the traditional notions of female passivity (Dalton & Asal, 2011; Weinberg & Eubank, 2011). On average women suicide bombers kill more people per event than their male counterparts (O'Rourke, 2009). Feminist scholars argue that essentialist rhetorics of male aggressor and female victim reinforce the images of women as powerless and devoid of agency. Denying the presence of agency shrinks

---

[4] Johnson (1997) explains that patriarchal societies promote male privilege by being male dominated, male identified and male centered. McIntosh (1988) explains privilege as an unearned advantage that is available to one social group and systematically denied to others. Moreover, within organized social systems a man's access to male privilege depends on related characteristics such as class, race, sexual orientation, ethnicity and disability status. She asserts that denial of men's accumulated advantages gained from women's accumulated disadvantage protects male privilege from being fully recognized, understood, addressed and eventually ended (McIntosh 1988). The cultural ideas like control, strength, decisiveness, rationality, self-sufficiency and logic are commonly associated with men and masculinity. These qualities are considered desirable, preferable and normal in contrast to those normally associated with women and femininity such as compassion, cooperation, caring, mutuality and sharing.

women's lives and choices to mere victimization. Contrary to popular images of women as passive victims of terrorism, research shows that women practice and exercise their agency as supporters, facilitators, perpetrators, participants, opposers, and survivors during conflict and terrorism (Alison, 2003, 2004; Dasgupta, 2009; Gunawardena, 2006; Parashar, 2011; Sjoberg, 2007; Sjoberg et al., 2011; Sjoberg & Gentry, 2007; Weinberg & Eubank, 2011).

Nevertheless, conflict and peace are inherently gendered processes. It is predominately men who fight wars and decide in favor of violence. The fact that women as victims and survivors carry disproportionate burden of war and conflict, including sexual violence, is well documented in conflict and peace literature (Cockburn, 2001; M'Cormack-Hale & M'Cormack-Hale, 2012; UN, 2004). This does not imply that given power women would not wage wars but it demonstrates that women's experience and understanding of peace and security is different from that of men. In fact there are numerous examples of how women find ways to resist and fight conditions of violence[5] (Anderlini, 2000; Caiazza, 2001). It is problematic to associate peace only with women and violence with men not only because women are capable of violence but because men can also be agents of non-violence and peace, like Mohandas Karamchand Ghandi, Nelson Mandela and Martin Luther King, Jr. What is problematic is the power asymmetry between men and women in most societies.

---

[5] There are a number of examples of women trying to rebuild their lives, of fighting state-sponsored and non-sponsored terrorism through their activism, in the Middle East, Latin America, and Northern Ireland. Andernili (2000) cites examples of women peace activism in Columbia, Georgia, Kashmir, Guatemala, Cyprus, Northern Ireland, Bosnia, Liberia, Rwanda, Burundi, and South Africa.

Due to the systematic power asymmetry between men and women across different societies, women have less access to power and resources (Kouvo & Levine, 2008). The United Nations (UN) acknowledges the exclusion of women in peace process and post conflict reconciliation processes in the Security Council Resolution 1350[6]. Although this resolution formally recognizes the gendered impacts of war and conflict on women and advocates for women's inclusion in post conflict peace negotiations, it fails to provide any substantial understanding of how gender inequality is a potential contributing factor to violence and terrorist acts. It is argued that including women in post conflict peace negotiation implies women's utility to peace rather than propagating overall women's equality to men (Charlesworth, 2008).

Analyzing women's role in conflict and peace, the primary focus should not be the narrow public sphere where women can act and have access to power but the large body of social, political, economic and cultural affairs where they are systematically deprived of participation and decision-making. In spite of a long history of women in the military, women are still a thin minority in military forces around the world with only a handful of women in higher decision-making positions[7]. Militaries around the world continue to be heavily male dominated with hyper-masculinized organizational and behavioral norms, where women are limited to non-combat supporting roles and men are

---

[6] Other key instruments include The Convention on the Elimination of All Forms of Discrimination against Women (1979), The Beijing Declaration and Platform for Action (1995) and United Nations Security Council Resolution 1325 on Women, Peace and Security (2000), Millennium Development Goals

[7] In 2011, women constituted 14.6% of the US active army, 18.5% of the Australian Defence Force, 8.5% of the Norwegian force and 8.55% of the French force. Women in combat are mostly in European countries such as Denmark, Estonia, Finland, France, Germany, Lithuania, Netherlands, Norway, Poland, Romania and Sweden. Other Angloshpere countries include Australia, Canada and New Zealand and only recently US has allowed women in combat. Outside Anglosphere includes Eritrea, Israel, and North Korea. Pakistan and South Africa allow women as fighter pilots (Fisher, 2013, January 25 ; Ratcliffe, 2011, December 8).

engaged in front line combat positions (Enloe, 2007)[8]. Some would argue that women involved in terrorism challenge the binary notions of cooperative women and conflictual men[9], however the available data shows that there are certainly more men in terrorist organizations than women (Mickolus, 1984). In spite of the recent rise in number of female terrorists, it is often men who are in leadership and decision making positions within terrorist organizations. While between 1985 and 2006, females represented fifteen percent of the number of suicide bombers (Schweitzer, 2006; Speckhard, 2008), none of these organizations had women in the top leadership positions, and all the suicide missions were designed and master minded by men (Berko & Erez, 2007). Even though some terrorist organizations promise a gender equality agenda, be it Chechen Black Widows, Palestinian female cadres or Birds of Paradise in LTTE, where women constitute about 30% of suicide attackers, women are still part of a cultural system that accords them unequal status.

Gender inequality continues to be a visible and persistent problem in all spheres of public life in most societies as observed by systematically collected national indicators ((WB), 2001; Hausmann, Tyson, & Zahidi, 2011). Gender discrimination remains pervasive in mostly all dimensions of life all over the world, with men dominating political, economic, social and religious institutions, and women and girls bearing the most direct and largest cost of inequalities. For instance in many countries women still lack the right to own land, manage property, and travel without escort or spousal consent. Women remain under represented in parliaments around the world, with the world

---

[8] Recently we are seeing reports of cases of sexual violence against women by and within militaries, which might have not been reported earlier due to stigma attached to rape (Dick, 2012; MacFarquhar, 2011).
[9] Caprioli and Boyer (2001) discuss these images in their paper 'Gender, Violence and International Crisis'

average of 20.4% in the parliament ((IPU), 2012). In most societies women are overrepresented in the informal sector leading to trends like feminization of poverty (Chen, 2001) they continue to face the glass ceiling effect, earn less than men (Arulampalam, Booth, & Bryan, 2007; Blau & Kahn, 2004), and working women bear a double burden of career and domestic /reproductive labor at home (Bratberg, Dahl, & Risa, 2002). Over all gender inequality indicators are a good proxy for social injustice and other kinds of inequalities for minorities and other disadvantaged groups in a society. In fact the notion of inequality is essentially linked to power asymmetry that provides advantage to one group over another. Conflict and political violence attenuate the differences in power thus further weakening those who are already without power. This power inequality is an important reason why gender equality matters for terrorism studies.

With regard to gender inequality and power asymmetry between men and women, the collective shared meaning and institutional setup in a society plays an important role in determining the opportunities and rights provided to women in a society. Lichbach (1997) theorizes this gap as the difference between subjective (i.e. individual values and attitudes) and the intersubjective (i.e. collective identity). Although individual attitudes contribute to collective identities, they do not fully constitute the collective institutional set up. As Ross (1997) explains that sharing a culture does not mean complete agreement on specifics by all the people; it only means that they share a similar worldview. Furthermore it is important to bear in mind that the effects of culture on collective action and political life are generally indirect.

Cultural perspectives only focus on expressed norms and views, while structural perspectives take into account actual practices and laws. The gap between culture and institutional structures suggests that institutional set up has a more direct impact on women's rights. Studies show that even in traditional societies, state interventions and institutional support can have a significant effect on facilitating women's empowerment (Htun, 2003; Kabeer & Stark, 2008). This implies that although culture is a powerful influence on gender equality, it is the collective institutional support that propels progress made in women's empowerment.

Hypotheses:

The above-mentioned discussion provides a board theoretical understanding of the connections between culture, gender inequality and terrorism. With regard to the gap between cultural attitudes and institutional support, we can hypothesize that actual outcomes of women's rights are a stronger measure of gender equality in a society. We can assume that the shared collective structure supporting gender equality, as reflected by actual outcomes, would have a more direct and stronger impact on terrorism, than individual beliefs and attitudes. Therefore I hypothesize that gender equality outcomes in education, employment and politics have a more direct and stronger impact on reducing terrorism than cultural attitudes for gender equality.

H1: Female literacy rates are a stronger deterrent to terrorism than cultural attitudes supporting women's right to education.

H2: Female labor force participation is a stronger deterrent to terrorism than cultural attitudes supporting women's right to work.

H3: Women's political participation is a stronger deterrent to terrorism than cultural attitudes supporting women's political rights.

3.3 Research Design

To test the above-mentioned hypotheses, this paper employs a cross-national times series estimation to check the relations between gender inequality and incidents of terrorism. It analyzes both gender equality attitudes and outcomes, with a range of controls.

Dependent Variable:

The dependent variable is the number of terrorist incidents in a country in a single year using Global Terrorism Database (GTD) (LaFree & Dugan, 2007). It is a publicly available, open- source and event-count database of aggregated domestic and international terrorist attacks from 1970 to 2010, for more than 200 countries and disputed areas. Scholarship fails to offer a concrete definition of terrorism, given its controversial nature. This study employs the definitional criteria set by GTD to record an event as a terrorist attack. The event has to be intentional, be violent or entail threat of it, carried out by non-state actors outside the realm of legitimate warfare. Also one of the two conditions must be fulfilled that the attack is carried out to influence a group larger than the immediate target and/ or the attack has a political, social, religious or ideological goal. A major limitation of the data is that it is based on open source information, and bias might be introduced if an event is not reported.

This paper demonstrates how domestic gender relations have an impact on state levels of terrorism and tests for both domestic and transnational terrorism separately. The decomposition of domestic and transnational terrorism is based on GTD data separated by Enders et al. (2011)[10]. Until recently scholarship has been debating the difference in the determinants of domestic and transnational terrorism. Most of the studies on determinants of terrorism focus on transnational terrorism (Enders & Sandler, 2000, 2002; Li, 2005; Li & Schaub, 2004; Piazza, 2008a; Robison, 2010). These studies focus on international terrorism because datasets on domestic terrorism, like GTD, have only recently become publically available. A recent study elucidates that domestic and transnational terrorism is driven by the same forces (Kis-Katos et al., 2011). Although the factors driving both domestic and international attacks might be similar, the theoretical causal explanations for both might be different. Past research shows that domestic terrorism can spill over to transnational terrorism, due to contagion effect and increased globalization (Enders et al., 2011; Midlarsky et al., 1980; Schmid, 2004).

Independent Variable- Gender Equality Cultural Attitudes:

Data on cultural attitudes towards gender equality comes from the World Values Survey (WVS) ("World Values Survey ", 2000) dataset. The WVS data is based on cross-national and longitudinal survey research programs carried out on a statistical sample in 97 countries[11] covering a period of 1981-2008 over six waves i.e. 1981-1984,

---

[10] Terrorism is domestic when terrorist act within their national boundary and when outside their national boundaries, it is international or transnational terrorism (Enders et al., 2011; Sánchez-Cuenca & de la Calle, 2009).

[11] The World Values Survey is a good mix of different kinds of societies at different levels of modernization based on the categorization of Human Development Index (HDI) produced annually by United Nations Development Program (UNDP). HDI is based on standard 100-point scale of societal modernization. WVS includes affluent market economies like Japan, United States and Switzerland, with per capita annual incomes as high as $40,000 or more, along with middle-level/ industrializing countries like Brazil, Taiwan and Turkey, and also agrarian societies such as Tanzania and Nigeria with per capita incomes of $300 or less. Based on Freedom House ratings of level of democracy, WVS includes data on older democracies like Canada, India, Australia; newer democracies like Taiwan, El-Salvador and Estonia;

1989-1993, 1994-1999, 1999-2004, 2005-2006, and 2008-2010. The model includes 57 countries over a period of 1994-2002, due to limited coverage of all variables of interest. (See in appendix 3-A for a list of the WVS countries included in this study).

Currently World Values Survey data is the best available pooled dataset recording cultural attitudes, basic values and beliefs of people. The major data limitation of WVS is the problem of external validity. This study includes only 57 countries from the WVS dataset, compared to the 200 countries covered by GTD. To test the similarity between the two groups of countries, a two independent samples t-test is conducted for levels of terrorism and various key social, economic and political indicators for WVS countries and rest of the countries, using Quality of Government data for 194 countries for the years 1994 and 2000. The test shows that the 57 countries in world value survey are overall not statistically representative of the rest of the countries in GTD (See appendix 3-B). There is a possible selection bias in the WVS sampling, which might be due to access to certain countries, such as political or logistical constraints. Thus the results of this study are limited to the 57 countries included in the world values survey. Another possible data limitation, as with any survey data, is the problem of measurement or response bias. There is a risk that the sample might differ from the true value of the corresponding population due to the method of observation.

The data is based on three survey questions that tap gender equality attitudes with regard to higher education, jobs and political participation (See appendix 3-C).

1. 'A university education is more important for a boy than a girl'

---

semi democracies like Turkey; non or controlled democracies like China, Zimbabwe and Jordon (Inglehart & Norris, 2003).

2. 'When jobs are scarce, men should have more right to a job than women'

3. 'On the whole, men make better political leaders than women do'

The survey questions use the interval-level response format. The first question uses three intervals i.e. 1 for agree, 2 for disagree and 3 for neither. The second and third questions use four intervals i.e. 1 for strongly agree, 2 for agree, 3 for disagree and 4 for strongly disagree. The author created dummy variables for the interval variables. The WVS is coded as individual level data so individual responses were converted to aggregates in a country year format. The percentages of the aggregates were employed to see how many people in a country agree or disagree. This analysis included dummy variables for cultural attitudes that support women's right to education, right to work and right to political participation.

Independent Variable – Gender Equality Actual Outcomes:

For the actual outcomes of female literacy rate, the variable of average years of education of women aged 25 and older in a country is used. The data is drawn from Gakidou, Cowling, Lozano, and Murray (2010). It covers the time period 1970-2009. The highest number of years in the sample is 13.6 years and lowest is 1.5 years, with an average of 8 years. This variable captures the institutional set up and progress made over the years to improve female education. It reflects the value placed on educating girls in a society; the level of resources employed and the provision of opportunities. Data on female labor force participation obtained from world development indicators (World Bank, 2003) is used to gauge actual levels of women's economic rights. It records the percentage of women ages 15 and above who are economically active during a specified period. It helps trace the structural changes in the labor force of a country over time, as more women join the labor force it reflects the changing social norms and customs. With regard to actual outcomes of women's political participation, the most appropriate variable is the percentage of women in parliament, which is relatively reliable and has good coverage. The data is taken from Melander (2005) which is originally drawn from the Inter-parliamentary union. It is available for 175 countries for the period 1965 to 2002. For bicameral parliament, the number of women in the upper house is recorded. It is a good measure for capturing the actual political participation and level of political empowerment of women in that society.

The state role in supporting women's rights is critical in providing institutional support and advancing women's rights in a country ((WB), 1995; Htun, 2003; Walsh, 2011). Therefore this model includes measures for institutional support and government practices towards women and how effectively it enforces laws supporting women's rights. The data for state support for economic rights and political rights is drawn from Cingranelli and Richards (2010) and it covers 199 countries for the period 1981-2008. Both the variables are ordinal, with a scale of 0 to 3, with 0 representing no rights for women, 1 is for few legal rights but poorly enforced by governments, 2 is where some rights are enforced and 3 represents countries where all women's rights are guaranteed by law. These variables provide valuable information about the different legal rights and protection extended to women by the government. The variable of women's social rights was not included because it is highly correlated with women's economic rights.

With regard to gender equality other useful measures are Gender-related Development Index (GDI) and Gender Empowerment Measure (GEM). However they were not included due to three reasons. First is the coverage issue, both variables are available only from 1995 onwards. Second, there are several conceptual problems with both the measures. GDI is not a measure of gender inequality but it is the Human Development Index (HDI) adjusted for gender disparities. And GEM does not provide sufficient information for comparisons across countries (Klasen, 2006). Third, the measures needed in this analysis were for women's progress in education, employment and political representation, to be compared to respective cultural attitudes. The GDI and GEM variables do not capture all the three elements that this paper examines.

Independent Variables – Controls:

Past literature has linked terrorism to domestic features like political regime, gross domestic product per capita, population size, number of conflicts a country has been involved in and a past terror incidents (Braithwaite & Li, 2007; Enders & Sandler, 2005; Feldmann & Perälä, 2004; Freytag et al., 2011; Li, 2005; Li & Schaub, 2004; Piazza, 2006, 2008a). Most of the control variables were drawn from Quality of Government dataset (Teorell, 2011). They include population size (Heston et al., 2009), real GDP per capita variable (Heston et al., 2009), and the polity i.e. the level of democracy (Marshall & Jaggers, 2002). The scale of level of democracy variable ranges from 0 to 10, with 10 being most democratic and 0 being least democratic. The past conflicts variable data is coded from the UCDP/PRIO Armed conflict dataset (Gleditsch et al., 2002). It is a count of the inter-state and intra-state conflicts the country is involved in a particular year. For the past terror incidents, the dependent variable is lagged by one year.

3.4 Estimation

This study employs pooled regression models using country-year data for 57 countries for the period 1994-2002, the full temporal range for which was available for all the variables employed in this study. The unit of analysis is an individual country in a single year.

The dependent variable is a count variable i.e. the number of terror attacks in a country in a particular year. It is strongly skewed to the right, as many countries that have never experienced any terror attack, and displays overdispersion[12]. It has a variance greater than the mean (See Table-3.1). In such cases the more suitable probability / regression model is a negative binomial model (Long & Freese, 2006). Previous studies with dependent variable that is a raw count of terrorist attacks in country-year format have also employed the negative binomial model (Brockhoff et al., 2010; Crenshaw & Robison, 2006; Lai, 2007a; Li & Schaub, 2004; Piazza, 2011; Piazza & Walsh, 2010; Robison, 2010). Robust standard errors are estimated to cope with heteroskedasticity and clustered by country to control for country specific variations. Problems of missing data occurred with the WVS data. The WVS is carried out in waves in different countries and the data is recorded only for the survey year in a particular country. To create a balanced data the value of the response in the survey year in a country is assigned over the entire WVS wave (See Table-3.1 for the descriptive statistics of the variables).

For robustness check to see whether women's actual rights are deterrents to terrorism even after a certain number of years. The actual women's rights variables i.e.

---

[12] Out of 305 total observations for terror attacks, 69 observations are zero.

female literacy rate, female labor force participation and women in the parliament, are lagged by 1 to 5 years to see the effects on terrorism incidents. Even after introducing the lags, women's actual progress in education, economic and political rights continue to be statistically significant and negative in relation to terrorism[13].

3.5 Interpretation

The results from this analysis are generally supportive of the hypotheses that actual outcomes of women's rights are stronger deterrents to terrorism than cultural attitudes for gender equality. The results indicate that states where actual outcomes of gender equality are low are more vulnerable to terror attacks.

Table-3.2 presents the impact of women's education attitudes and outcomes on terrorism. Actual outcome of years of female education is negative and statistically significant in relation to overall terrorism (Table-3.2, Model-3), domestic terrorism (Table-3.2, Model-6) and transnational terrorism (Table-3.2, Model-9). This supports the first hypothesis that actual outcomes of women's education level i.e. female literacy level, deters terrorist attacks. Cultural attitudes towards women's education are neither statistically significant nor negative in any of the models in Table-3.2. A 1% increase in female years of education would result in about 23% reduction in overall terrorism. Similarly a 1% increase in this variable lowers domestic terrorism by about 21%, and transnational terrorism by about 18%. On average if a country experienced 22 attacks during 1994-2002, lowering terrorism by 23% means 5 less attacks per year.

---

[13] The results are available with author and can be shared upon request.

The empirical evidence by Bravo and Dias (2006) and Azam and Thelen (2008) shows association between low levels of education and more terrorism. On the other hand there is also evidence that individual terrorists are better educated than national averages[14] (Benmelech & Berrebi, 2007; Hassan, 2001, November 19; Krueger & Male ková, 2003). Krueger and Maleckova make the argument that perhaps terrorists are more educated but come from countries with lower levels of education. The results suggest women's education level has an impact on terrorism. This finding is contrary to Brockhoff et al. (2010), who did not find any direct links between overall education and terrorism. This difference could be due to the reason that they were looking at overall enrollment rates and literacy levels, which do not necessarily capture the gender inequalities present within overall national statistics. This supports the paper's argument that traditional indicators are insufficient to capture gender inequality patterns in a country, making it imperative to have gender disaggregated data for all spheres of life.

Looking at outcomes and attitudes with regard to women's economic rights and their impact on terrorism, the results confirm the second hypothesis, which states that female labor force participation is a stronger deterrent to terrorism than cultural attitudes supporting women's right to work. Table-3.3 shows that a 1% increase in female labor force participation lowers terrorism by about 11% (Model-3) and domestic terrorism by about 10.95% (Model-6). For transnational terrorism we see that both attitudes and outcomes have a significant and negative impact on terrorism (Table-3.3, Model-9). But

---

[14] See Hassan, Nasra (2001, November 19). An Arsenal of Believers: Talking to the "human bombs' The New Yorker. Retrieved from http://www.newyorker.com/archive/2001/11/19/011119fa_FACT1

outcomes appear to be stronger deterrents than attitudes. While a 1% increase in female labor force participation lowers transnational terrorism by 8.9%, a 1% increase in attitudes supporting women's right to work lowers terrorism only by 2.85%. Outcomes turn out to be more effective in lowering terrorism, generally supporting Hypothesis-2. Robison (2010) also found empirical evidence that higher levels of women's economic empowerment is associated with lower transnational terrorism.

Next Table-3.4 presents the impact of women's political participation, actual outcomes versus attitudes, on terrorism. Results show that although both attitudes and outcomes are significant, only actual outcomes are negatively associated with terrorism[15]. A 1% increase in number of women in the parliament leads to a 5.6% decrease in terrorism (Table-3.4, Model-3), and a 6.2% decrease in domestic terrorism (Table-3.4, Model-6). The results are unexpected for transnational terrorism, where outcomes are not statistically significant. This means that women's political rights have no impact on lowering transnational terror attacks. In fact attitudes are significant, and positively related to terrorism, domestic and transnational, which mean that higher the public support for women's political rights, the more terrorism is experienced. This probably is due to high levels of gap between attitudes and actual results of women's political rights in many countries. On average about 50% of people in the world values survey support women's political rights, but on average percentage of women in the parliament is only 11% (see Table-3.1). So even if there is high attitudinal support for women's rights, it is

---

[15] In a previous study I find that the women in parliament variable is statistically significant and negative in association to transnational terrorism. The basic difference is the number of countries examined. My previous study included a bigger sample of 155 countries (from 1981 to 2002), and this study includes only 57 countries (from 1994 to 2002) due to data constraints of World Values Survey.

not sufficient to insulate the society against terrorism, unless there is corresponding actual advancement in women's political participation. This suggests that mere verbal or attitudinal support without equivalent and necessary action to support women's rights is not sufficient to establish a peaceful society.

It also means that the WVS survey question about supporting women's political rights is not analogous to more women in the parliament. Political rights might also include participation in politics, representation in political parties, right to be elected and women's representation in local governments. Political rights capture a broader understanding of women's political role than just the number of women in the parliament. The objective of this study was to test whether outcomes or attitudes are a better deterrent to terrorism. The results show that outcomes of women's political rights are negatively related to terrorism, suggesting that outcomes are better deterrents of terrorism.

With regard to control variables, overall the variable of past incidents is statistically significant and positive at 0.05 level in all models. It means that if a country experienced terrorism in the previous year, there is higher probability of more terror attacks in the next year. Also population is seen as positive and statistically significant in models looking at women's economic rights (Table-3.3). This implies that bigger populations are more prone to terror attack, which could be because larger countries are harder to police (Eyerman, 1998) or that larger countries are more heterogeneous and alienated segments might resort to terrorism to influence governments (Li & Schaub, 2004).

The distinction between outcomes and attitudes is critical, especially with regard to gender equality, because assuming that gender equality attitudes reflect what people actually do in practice is problematic. This awareness is important for effective counterterrorism policies to avoid any reverse and undesired consequences. Societies have discrepancies in what people report believing and what they actually do; what is intended and how they act. Also there can be a gap in what people want and what is structurally and institutionally possible. This gap draws attention to the problem of structural and institutional barriers to peoples' aspirations. It ties in with Lichbach's (1997) framework of subjective and intersubjective culture, of the gap between individual attitudes and shared meaning and the collective social structures. This understanding provides a useful framework in similar debates about social justice in societies.

3.6 Conclusion

The evidence presented here, suggests that positive gender equality outcomes are deterrents to terrorism. This study provides a statistical foundation to future research on the relationship between terrorism and cultural attitudes. It contributes to our understanding of how attitudes as well as outcomes affect terrorism and has tremendous policy implications for focusing on gender equality outcomes to deter terrorism. Gender equality is indicative of power asymmetry between men and women, and it is also a good proxy of other inequalities prevalent in a society that denies justice and access to power to disadvantaged groups. It implies that progress in gender equality builds a more just and inclusive society, dissipating feelings of deprivation, frustration and hopelessness that drives people and groups to choose violence over peaceful means of protest and conflict resolution.

In light of these results there is need to revisit policy perspectives that ignore the distinction between cultural attitudes and actual outcomes. This study confirms an important gap between the attitudes people have and the actual outcomes on the ground, especially with regard to gender equality. The gap might be due to discrepancies between what people say and what they actually do, or due to institutional, structural and social barriers to realizing what one wants to achieve. Outcomes capture the presence of state policies, access to rights and agency to exercise those rights. Attitudes, on the other hand, are limited to opinions regarding those rights. These findings challenge the rhetoric that changing attitudes fixes issues of inequality. Attitudes are difficult to measure and hard to shape and change with outside interventions. Designing anti-terrorism strategies on the assumption of attitudes reflecting actual situation on ground can be misleading and problematic. On the other hand actual outcomes are more tangible and visible, relatively measureable and can be addressed by appropriate policy interventions. This research has a broad applicability to other areas of policy interventions, which rely on cultural attitudes as measure of change.

It is recognized that the major limitation of this paper is generalizibility of results to countries not included in the analysis. For the 57 countries included in the study, for the time period 1994-2002, it becomes clear that gender equality outcomes are deterrents and determinants of terrorism. There is indeed no 'one size fits all' as each country's specific condition and local context influence its security context and responses but the empirical results suggest taking gender inequality issues into account can initiate a productive discussion on approaches to and understanding of security and peace. So far this is missing in the dominant discourse on understanding determinants of terrorism. The strength of this study is that it helps unveil the complex interactions between attitudes and outcomes and their impact on terrorism. It looks at panel data and controls for country variations and studies trends over time. A cross-national time series analysis provides the unique opportunity to observe patterns of gender equality determinants of terrorism.

Although we still do not have enough evidence to make a causal argument for higher gender equality lowering terrorism, the empirical evidence in this paper supports for the views captured in the theoretical model presented above. There is growing recognition that gender equality matters in both theory and practice of security studies (Caprioli & Boyer, 2001; Caprioli et al., 2007; Hudson, 2012; Hudson et al., 2008; Sjoberg et al., 2011; Tickner, 1992), yet more rigorous research is needed to firmly establish the causal patterns between gender equality and terrorism. A major hurdle in this regard is the paucity of gender-disaggregated data. There is need for data collection on how women are affected by terrorism, as participants, victims, survivors and peace activists. In fact gender segregated data is needed in all aspects of life, for instance the data on female labor participation covers any kind of paid job, and does not separate high and low paid jobs. In countries where women are over-represented in low paid jobs, feminization of poverty is a critical issue.

Further research should focus on the household decision-making power and access to resources between men and women and how that impacts terrorism. More research is needed to explore the relationship between feminization of poverty and terrorism. Another important area is the kind of education provided in schools to boys and girls and its links to terrorism, as it is not just years of education but also the content of education that impacts terrorism. Also there is need for studies that look at the relationship of women's peace movements and its impact on terrorism. With regard to political rights, future studies can explore women's role in local government as deterrents to domestic terrorism.

Gender equality has promise to provide a sustainable bulwark against circumstances that breed terrorism. In order to mitigate systematic gender inequality there is need for rigorous and direct challenge to the deeply embedded gender ideologies, notions and norms. Many countries have employed quotas to enhance women's equal participation in public life, which has secured concrete gains over time. Quotas are an efficient mechanism to correct the under-representation of women, but their use is limited to just increasing numbers[16]. If women continue to be tokens in parliaments, gender equality meets a dead-end when the notion of equal opportunity fails to develop into the equality of results in other spheres of life. This demands a coordinated, multi-disciplinary and systematic policy response as given its complexity and magnitude; no single intervention can deter terrorism.

---

[16] Quota project: Global database of quotas for women. See http://www.quotaproject.org/aboutQuotas.cfm

Appendix 3-A

List of countries in world values survey (1994-2002)

Sr no	Country code	Country name
1.	2	United States
2.	20	Canada
3.	42	Dominican Republic
4.	70	Mexico
5.	92	El Salvador
6.	100	Colombia
7.	101	Venezuela
8.	135	Peru
9.	140	Brazil
10.	155	Chile
11.	160	Argentina
12.	165	Uruguay
13.	230	Spain
14.	255	Germany
15.	290	Poland
16.	310	Hungary
17.	316	Czech Republic
18.	317	Slovakia
19.	339	Albania
20.	343	Macedonia
21.	344	Croatia
22.	346	Bosnia and Herzegovina
23.	349	Slovenia
24.	355	Bulgaria
25.	359	Moldova
26.	360	Romania
27.	366	Estonia
28.	367	Latvia
29.	368	Lithuania
30.	369	Ukraine
31.	370	Belarus

32.	371	Armenia
33.	372	Georgia
34.	373	Azerbaijan
35.	375	Finland
36.	380	Sweden
37.	385	Norway
38.	475	Nigeria
39.	510	Tanzania
40.	552	Zimbabwe
41.	560	South Africa
42.	600	Morocco
43.	615	Algeria
44.	630	Iran
45.	640	Turkey
46.	651	Egypt
47.	663	Jordan
48.	703	Kyrgyzstan
49.	710	China
50.	732	Korea, South
51.	740	Japan
52.	750	India
53.	771	Bangladesh
54.	830	Singapore
55.	840	Philippines
56.	850	Indonesia
57.	900	Australia

Appendix 3-B

Comparing 57 WVS and non-WVS countries using QOG

	Variables	1994			2000		
		Mean of non-WVS countries	Mean of WVS countries	Mean comparison (t-test)	Mean of non-WVS countries	Mean of WVS countries	Mean comparison (t-test)
1	Terror attacks	4.1794 (9.454)	27.461 (51.556)	-4.771***	2.076 (6.106)	10.756 (26.865)	-3.370***
2	Domestic attacks	1.854 (3.857)	17.576 (33.740)	-4.997***	0.957 (3.747)	6.1025 (16.785)	-3.202***
3	Transnational attacks	1.3846 (4.979)	4.4487 (9.757)	-2.882***	0.419 (1.385)	0.654 (1.885)	-1.002
4	Average Years of Education (Female)	4.271 (3.180)	6.9272 (3.4271)	-5.205***	4.953 (3.402)	7.714 (3.502)	-5.170***
5	% Labor Force Participation (Female)	38.132 (8.923)	39.943 (8.255)	-1.321	38.895 (8.118)	40.9118 (7.384)	-1.629
6	% Women in parliament	8.76710 (7.730)	10.0027 (8.1104)	-0.952	12.3868 (9.8414)	13.012 (9.2547)	-0.400
7	State support for women's economic rights	1.217 (0.565)	1.36 (0.6706)	1.373	1.30555 (0.597)	1.3866 (0.613)	-0.812
8	State support for women's political rights	1.543 (0.716)	1.803 (0.517)	-2.527***	1.7222 (0.676)	2.00 (0.462)	-2.932***
9	Polity	5.7083 (3.490)	6.6292 (2.997)	-1.879*	5.842 (3.382)	7.150 (2.813)	-2.789***
10	Real GDP/capita	8082.95 (10712.2)	10326.02 (8975.9)	-1.482	9262.773 (12399.6)	12281.77 (10661.9)	-1.708*
11	Population (thousands)	5434.16 (7362.85)	59324.22 (171302)	-3.176***	6184.757 (8463.80)	63997.27 (184403.6)	-3.164***
12	Conflict	0.241 (0.528)	0.299 (0.844)	-0.527	0.219 (0.492)	0.286 (1.011)	-0.551

Standard deviation is in the parenthesis ( )
*** ($p < 0.01$), **($p < 0.05$), *($p < 0.10$) (two–tailed)

Appendix 3-C

World Values Survey questions

Do you agree, disagree or neither agree nor disagree with the following statements? (Read out and code one answer for each statement):

V44. When jobs are scarce, men should have more right to a job than women.

    Agree   1
    Disagree   2
    Neither   3

V61. On the whole, men make better political leaders than women do.

    Strongly agree   1
    Agree   2
    Disagree   3
    Strongly disagree 4

V62. A university education is more important for a boy than for a girl.

    Strongly agree   1
    Agree   2
    Disagree   3
    Strongly disagree 4

Table 3.1: Descriptive statistics of variables in country-year format for 57 countries (1994-2002)

Variables	Source	Mean	Standard Deviation
Terrorist Incidents	Global Terrorism Database	22.38	52.72
Domestic terrorism	Global Terrorism Database	14.393	35.125
Transnational terrorism	Global Terrorism Database	3.32	12.402
% Attitude supporting women's higher education	World Values Survey	75.03	10.778
% Attitude supporting women's jobs	World Values Survey	41.25	20.64
% Attitude supporting women's political leadership	World Values Survey	50.157	17.37
Average Years of Education (Female)	Gakidou, Cowling, Lozano, and Murray (2010)	8.02	2.984
% Labor Force Participation (Female)	World Bank (2003)	40.83	6.36
% Women in parliament	Inter parliamentary union ((IPU))	11.02	8.53
Women's economic rights	CIRI-(Cingranelli and Richards, 2010)	1.42	.59
Women's political rights	CIRI-(Cingranelli and Richards, 2010)	1.97	.42
Polity	Marshall & Jaggers (2002)	7.30	2.38
Real GDP/capita	Heston, Summers, & Aten (2009)	10850.36	9361.67
Population (thousands)	Heston, Summers, & Aten (2009)	98566.92	245367
Conflict	UCDP/PRIO Armed conflict dataset	.4131	1.19
Past Incidents	Global Terrorism Database	20.06	51.04

binomial regression comparing effects of cultural attitudes and actual outcomes of women's ... nts within 57 countries (1994-2002)

	Terrorism Incidents			Domestic Terrorism			Transnational Terrorism		
	Model 1	Model 2	Model 3	Model 4	Model 5	Model 6	Model 7	Model 8	Model 9
	0.020		0.013	0.020		0.012	0.026		0.016
	(0.016)		(0.012)	(0.016)		(0.013)	(0.020)		(0.020)
		-0.275***	-0.262***		-0.257***	-0.244***		-0.225***	-0.203*
		(0.070)	(0.063)		(0.072)	(0.066)		(0.094)	(0.084)
	-0.010	0.183	0.165	-0.123	0.021	0.019	0.398	0.604*	0.544
	(0.291)	0.257	(0.248)	(0.261)	(0.225)	(0.217)	(0.350)	0.348	(0.338)
	-0.448	-0.142	-0.213	-0.589	-0.254	-0.321	-0.480	-0.273	-0.359
	(0.572)	(0.534)	(0.530)	(0.652)	(0.617)	(0.613)	(0.570)	(0.559)	(0.575)
	0.154	0.132	0.128	0.126	0.105	0.100	0.128	0.169	0.160
	(0.126)	(0.107)	(0.103)	(0.127)	(0.112)	(0.108)	(0.125)	(0.120)	(0.120)
	-0.00003	0.00003	0.00003	-0.00002	0.00004	0.00003	-0.00003	5.17e-06	-8.60e-
	(0.00002)	(0.00003)	(0.00002)	(0.00003)	(0.00003)	(0.00003)	(0.00003)	(0.00003)	(0.000)
	1.17e-06	5.02e-07	4.97e-07	1.12e-06	4.89e-07	4.95e-07	9.91e-07	6.12e-07	5.88e-0
	(1.03e-06)	(9.40e-07)	9.16e-07	(9.92e-07)	(9.54e-07)	9.22e-07	(1.15e-06)	(1.13e-06)	(1.12e-
	0.422	0.384	0.397	0.424	0.394	0.402	0.495	0.394	0.430
	(0.445)	(0.413)	(0.396)	(0.444)	(0.413)	(0.394)	(0.526)	(0.547)	(0.538)
	0.018**	0.012**	0.012**	0.017**	0.011**	0.011**	0.015**	0.013**	0.013*
	(0.005)	(0.003)	(0.004)	(0.005)	(0.003)	(0.004)	(0.005)	(0.004)	(0.004)
	0.506	2.876	2.052	0.613	2.885	2.112	-2.159	0.287	-0.686
	(1.532)	(1.321)	(1.349)	(1.641)	(1.458)	(1.534)	(1.635)	(1.406)	(1.738)
	305	305	305	305	305	305	305	305	305
	-1036.24	-1017.30	-1016.46	-896.76	-882.57	-882.01	-531.91	-527.42	-526.78

adjusted over countries, in parentheses.
rcent ($p < 0.01$), **Significance at 5 percent ($p < 0.05$), *Significance at 10 percent $p < 0.10$ (two–tailed)

Negative binomial regression comparing effects of cultural attitudes and actual outcomes of women[...] terrorist attack counts within 57 countries (1994-2001)

Variables	Terrorism Incidents			Domestic terrorism			Transnational terror[...]	
	Model 1	Model 2	Model 3	Model 4	Model 5	Model 6	Model 7	Model 8
[-ing]	-0.009 (0.011)		-0.013 (0.012)	-0.007 (0.011)		-0.013 (0.012)	-0.031*** (0.009)	
[-cipation]		-.0118*** (0.031)	-0.118*** (0.029)		-0.114*** (0.030)	-0.116*** (0.029)		-0.113*** (0.031)
[women's]	0.123 (0.328)	0.190 (0.314)	0.307 (0.326)	-0.030 (0.283)	0.015 (0.296)	0.137 (0.293)	0.921*** (0.339)	0.655* (0.375)
[men's]	-0.343 (0.586)	-0.321 0.529	-0.290 (0.518)	-0.497 (0.658)	-0.472 (0.598)	-0.450 (0.581)	-0.217 (0.510)	0.240 (0.551)
	0.153 (0.143)	0.189* 0.097)	0.185* (0.096)	0.127 (0.142)	0.174* (0.100)	0.169* (0.098)	0.091 (0.125)	0.173 (0.108)
	-0.00001 0.00003)	-0.00002 (0.00002)	-7.96e-06 (0.00003)	-3.07e-06 (0.00003)	-0.00001 (0.00002)	8.98e-07 (0.00003)	4.61e-06 (0.00003)	-0.00003 0.00002)
[-ds)]	1.18e-06 (1.02e-06)	1.95e-06** (8.68e-07)	2.00e-06*** (7.61e-07)	1.12e-06 (1.03e-06)	1.94e-06** (8.80e-07)	2.01e-06*** (7.70e-07)	1.01e-06 (9.46e-07)	1.62e-06 (1.01e-06)
	0.422 0.472	0.183 (0.440)	0.150 (0.396)	0.431 (0.485)	0.186 (0.443)	0.147 (0.392)	0.408 (0.425)	0.216 (0.546)
	0.017** (0.006)	0.014*** (0.003)	0.013*** (0.004)	0.016*** (0.006)	0.013*** (0.003)	0.012*** (0.004)	0.013*** (0.005)	0.014*** (0.003)
	1.795 (1.496)	5.887 (2.026)	6.102 (1.982)	1.909 (1.615)	5.850 (2.054)	6.181 (2.065)	-0.332 (1.209)	3.194 (1.947)
	305	305	305	305	305	305	305	305
[-od]	-1037.08	-1019.76	-1017.52	-897.80	-883.33	-881.43	-523.50	-523.87

[...]rors, adjusted over countries, in parentheses.
[...]t 1 percent (p < 0.01), **Significance at 5 percent ($p < 0.05$), *Significance at 10 percent $p < 0.10$ (two–tailed)

Negative binomial regression comparing effects of cultural attitudes and actual outcomes of women's counts within 57 countries (1994-2001)

	Terrorism Incidents			Domestic terrorism			Transnational terrorism		
	Model 1	Model 2	Model 3	Model 4	Model 5	Model 6	Model 7	Model 8	Model 9
	0.029***		0.031***	0.030**		0.031***	0.043***		0.043***
	(0.010)		(0.010)	(0.010)		(0.011)	(0.016)		(0.016)
		-0.054**	-0.058**		-0.060**	-0.064**		-0.014	-0.003
		(0.027)	(0.027)		(0.027)	(0.028)		(0.052)	(0.043)
	-0.099	0.164	-0.006	-0.179	0.055	-0.076	0.225	0.513	0.232
	(0.296)	(0.283)	(0.276)	(0.281)	(0.258)	(0.267)	(0.354)	(0.372)	(0.359)
	-0.505	0.108	-0.009	-0.674	0.042	-0.095	-0.748	-0.250	-0.720
	(0.541)	(0.637)	(0.574)	(0.616)	(0.717)	(0.654)	(0.527)	(0.617)	(0.571)
	0.123	0.174	0.145	0.098	0.158	0.132	0.107	0.144	0.108
	(0.114)	(0.143)	(0.118)	(0.108)	(0.150)	(0.118)	(0.107)	(0.135)	(0.113)
	-0.00004*	-0.00002	-0.00004*	-0.00003	-8.28e-06	-0.00003	-0.00006**	-0.00002	-0.00006*
	(0.00002)	(0.00002)	(0.00002)	(0.00002)	(0.00002)	(0.00002)	(0.00003)	(0.00003)	(0.00003)
	1.09e-06	1.74e-06	1.65e-06	1.08e-06	1.78e-06	1.73e-06	8.92e-07	1.28e-06	9.27e-07
	(9.58e-07)	(1.36e-06)	(1.18e-06)	(8.97e-07)	(1.39e-06)	(1.18e-06)	(9.77e-07)	(1.70e-06)	(1.33e-06)
	0.382	0.483	0.415	0.375	0.480	0.403	0.360	0.513	0.366
	(0.402)	(0.585)	(0.490)	(0.391)	(0.610)	(0.501)	(0.451)	(0.672)	(0.493)
	0.017***	0.018***	0.017**	0.016**	0.017**	0.016***	0.013***	0.016***	0.013***
	(0.006)	(0.005)	(0.006)	(0.006)	(0.005)	(0.006)	(0.005)	(0.005)	(0.005)
	1.108	0.837	0.241	1.195	0.811	0.165	-1.131	-0.923	-1.176
	(1.214)	(1.749)	(1.428)	(1.337)	(1.916)	(1.576)	(1.076)	(1.715)	(1.292)
	305	305	305	305	305	305	305	305	305
	-1030.34	-1034.18	-1025.03	-891.27	-894.18	-885.97	-523.75	-533.75	-523.74

adjusted over countries, in parentheses.
percent ($p < 0.01$), **Significance at 5 percent ($p < 0.05$), *Significance at 10 percent $p < 0.10$ (two–tailed)

References:

(IPU), Inter-Parliamentary Union. (2012). Women in National Parliaments. Retrieved October 2012 www.ipu.org\wmn-e\world.htm

(WB), World Bank. (1995). Toward gender equality : the role of public policy. Washington, D.C.: World Bank.

(WB), World Bank. (2001). Engendering Development through Gender Equality in Rights, Resources, and Voice. New York, NY.

Abadie, Alberto. (2006). Poverty, Political Freedom, and the Roots of Terrorism. *The American Economic Review, 96*(2), 50-56.

Alison, Miranda. (2003). Cogs in the Wheel? Women in the Liberation Tigers of Tamil Eelam. *Civil Wars, 6*(4), 37-54. doi: 10.1080/1369824042000221367

Alison, Miranda. (2004). Women as Agents of Political Violence: Gendering Security. *Security Dialogue, 35*(4), 447-463. doi: 10.1177/0967010604049522

Anderlini, Sanam Naraghi. (2000). Women at the peace table. New York: UN Development Fund for Women.

Anderson, Mark Cronlund. (2011). The U.S. Frontier Myth, American Identity and 9/11. *Journal of Psychohistory, 38*(4), 314-327.

Arulampalam, Wiji, Booth, Alison L, & Bryan, Mark L. (2007). Is there a glass ceiling over Europe? Exploring the gender pay gap across the wage distribution. *Industrial and Labor Relations Review*, 163-186.

Atkeson, Lonna Rae, & Rapoport, Ronald B. (2003). The More Things Change The More They Stay The Same: Examining Gender Differences In Political Attitude Expression, 1952--2000. *Public Opinion Quarterly, 67*(4), 495-521.

Azam, Jean-Paul, & Thelen, Véronique. (2008). The Roles of Foreign Aid and Education in the War on Terror. *Public Choice, 135*(3/4), 375-397. doi: 10.2307/27698274

Beer, Caroline. (2009). Democracy and Gender Equality. *Studies in Comparative International Development, 44*(3), 212-227.

Benmelech, Efraim, & Berrebi, Claude. (2007). Human capital and the productivity of suicide bombers. *The Journal of Economic Perspectives, 21*(3), 223-238.

Berko, Anat, & Erez, Edna. (2007). Gender, Palestinian Women, and Terrorism: Women's Liberation or Oppression? *Studies in Conflict & Terrorism, 30*(6), 493-519. doi: 10.1080/10576100701329550

Berrebi, Claude, & Ostwald, Jordan. (2013). Terrorism and the Labor Force. *RAND Working paper*.

Bjarnegård, Elin, & Melander, Erik. (2011). Disentangling gender, peace and democratization: the negative effects of militarized masculinity. *Journal of Gender Studies, 20*(2), 139-154. doi: 10.1080/09589236.2011.565194

Blau, Francine D, & Kahn, Lawrence M. (2004). The US gender pay gap in the 1990s: Slowing convergence: National Bureau of Economic Research.

Braithwaite, Alex, & Li, Quan. (2007). Transnational Terrorism Hot Spots: Identification and Impact Evaluation. *Conflict Management and Peace Science, 24*(4), 281-296. doi: http://cmp.sagepub.com/archive/

Bratberg, Espen, Dahl, Svenn Åge, & Risa, Alf Erling. (2002). 'The Double Burden': Do Combinations of Career and Family Obligations Increase Sickness Absence among Women? *European Sociological Review, 18*(2), 233-249.

Bravo, Ana Bela Santos, & Dias, Carlos Manuel Mendes (2006). An Empirical Analysis Of Terrorism: Deprivation, Islamism And Geopolitical Factors. *Defence & Peace Economics, 17*(4), 329-341. doi: 10.1080/10242690500526509

Brockhoff, Sarah, Krieger, Tim, & Meierrieks, Daniel. (2010). Ties That Do Not Bind (Directly): The Education-Terrorism Nexus Revisited. from CIE Center for International Economics

Caiazza, Amy. (2001). Why gender matters in understanding September 11: Women, militarism, and violence *Publication no. 1908*. Washington, DC: Institute for Women's Policy Research.

Caprioli, Mary. (2000). Gendered Conflict. *Journal of Peace Research, 37*(1), 51-68.

Caprioli, Mary. (2003). Gender Equality and State Aggression: The Impact of Domestic Gender Equality on State First Use of Force. *International Interactions, 29*(3), 195.

Caprioli, Mary. (2005). Primed for Violence: The Role of Gender Inequality in Predicting Internal Conflict. *International Studies Quarterly, 49*(2), 161-178.

Caprioli, Mary, & Boyer, Mark A. (2001). Gender, Violence, and International Crisis. *The Journal of Conflict Resolution, 45*(4), 503-518.

Caprioli, Mary, Emmett, Chad, Hudson, Valerie M. , Spanvill, Bonnie Ballif-, & McDermott, Rose. (2007). Putting women in their place. *Baker Center Journal of Applied Public Policy, 1*(1), 12- 24.

Charlesworth, Hilary. (2008). Are Women Peaceful? Reflections on the Role of Women in Peace-Building. *Feminist Legal Studies, 16*(3), 347-361. doi: 10.1007/s10691-008-9101-6

Chen, Martha Alter. (2001). Women and informality: A global picture, the global movement. *sais Review, 21*(1), 71-82.

Cingranelli, David L., & Richards, David L. (2010). The Cingranelli and Richards (CIRI) Human Rights Data Project. *Human Rights Quarterly, 32*(2), 401-424.

Cockburn, C. (2001). The gendered dynamics of armed conflict and political violence. In C. Moser & F. C. Clark (Eds.), *Victims, perpetrators or actors* (pp. 13-29). London: Zed.

Crenshaw, Edward M., & Robison, Kristopher K. (2006). Globalization and the Digital Divide: The Roles of Structural Conduciveness and Global Connection in Internet Diffusion. *Social Science Quarterly (Blackwell Publishing Limited), 87*(1), 190-207. doi: 10.1111/j.0038-4941.2006.00376.x

Crenshaw, Martha. (1981). The Causes of Terrorism. *Comparative Politics, 13*(4), 379-399.

Croson, Rachel, & Gneezy, Uri. (2009). Gender differences in preferences. *Journal of Economic Literature*, 448-474.

Dalton, Angela, & Asal, Victor. (2011). Is It Ideology or Desperation: Why Do Organizations Deploy Women in Violent Terrorist Attacks? *Studies in Conflict & Terrorism, 34*(10), 802-819. doi: 10.1080/1057610x.2011.604833

Dasgupta, Rajashri. (2009). Women Doing Peace. *Economic and Political Weekly, 44*(9), 31-33. doi: 10.2307/40278550

deBoer, Connie. (1985). The polls: The European peace movement and deployment of nuclear missiles. *The Public Opinion Quarterly, 49*(1), 119-132.

Dhillon, Navtej. (2008). Middle East Youth Bulge: Challenge or Opportunity? *Presentation to Congressional staff, 22*.

Dick, Kirby (Producer). (2012). The invisible war [Documentary] Retrieved from http://invisiblewarmovie.com/

Dietz, Mary G. (1985). I. Citizenship with a Feminist Face: The Problem with Maternal Thinking. *Political Theory, 13*(1), 19-37. doi: 10.1177/0090591785013001003

Eager, Paige Whaley. (2008). *From freedom fighters to terrorists: women and political violence*: Ashgate Publishing Company.

Eagly, Alice H., & Diekman, Amanda B. . (2006). *Examining gender gaps in sociopolitical attitudes: It's not Mars and Venus*. Working Paper Series. Institute for Policy Research Northwestern University.

Eagly, Alice H., Diekman, Arnanda B., Johannesen-schmidt, Mary C., & Koenig, Anne M. (2004). Gender Gaps in Sociopolitical Attitudes: A Social Psychological Analysis. *Journal of Personality & Social Psychology, 87*(6), 796-816.

Eichenberg, Richard C, & Stoll, Richard J. (2012). Gender Difference or Parallel Publics? The Dynamics of Defense Spending Opinions in the United States, 1965–2007. *Journal of Conflict Resolution, 56*(2), 331-348.

Elshtain, Jean Bethke. (1985). II. Reflections on War and Political Discourse: Realism, Just War, and Feminism in a Nuclear Age. *Political Theory, 13*(1), 39-57. doi: 10.1177/0090591785013001004

Enders, Walter, & Sandler, Todd. (2000). Is Transnational Terrorism Becoming More Threatening? A Time-Series Investigation. *The Journal of Conflict Resolution, 44*(3), 307-332.

Enders, Walter, & Sandler, Todd. (2002). Patterns of Transnational Terrorism, 1970-1999: Alternative Time-Series Estimates. *International Studies Quarterly, 46*(2), 145-165.

Enders, Walter, & Sandler, Todd. (2005). Transnational Terrorism 1968-2000: Thresholds, Persistence, and Forecasts. *Southern Economic Journal, 71*(3), 467-482.

Enders, Walter, Sandler, Todd, & Gaibulloev, Khusrav. (2011). Domestic versus transnational terrorism: Data, decomposition, and dynamics. *Journal of Peace Research, 48*(3), 319-337. doi: 10.1177/0022343311398926

Enloe, Cynthia. (2007). *Globalization and Militarism; Feminists Make the Link*: Rowman & Littlefield Publishers, Inc.

Eubank, William, & Weinberg, Leonard. (2001). Terrorism and Democracy: Perpetrators and Victims. *Terrorism and Political Violence, 13*(1), 155-164. doi: 10.1080/09546550109609674

Eyerman, Joe. (1998). Terrorism and democratic states: Soft targets or accessible systems. *International Interactions, 24*(2), 151-170. doi: 10.1080/03050629808434924

Farr, Vanessa. (2002). Gendering Demilitarization as a Peacebuilding Tool, paper 20. *Bonn, Bonn International Centre for Conversion (BICC)*, 14-24.

Feldmann, Andreas E., & Pera la , Maiju. (2004). Reassessing the Causes of Nongovernmental Terrorism in Latin America. *Latin American Politics and Society, 46*(2), 101-132.

Fisher, Max (2013, January 25). Map: Which countries allow women in front-line combat roles?, *The Washington Post* Retrieved from http://www.washingtonpost.com/blogs/worldviews/wp/2013/01/25/map-which-countries-allow-women-in-front-line-combat-roles/

Fite, David, Genest, Marc, & Wilcox, Clyde. (1990a). Gender Differences in Foreign Policy Attitudes. *American Politics Research, 18*(4), 492-513. doi: 10.1177/1532673x9001800406

Fite, David, Genest, Marc, & Wilcox, Clyde. (1990b). GENDER DIFFERENCES IN FOREIGN POLICY ATTITUDES. *American Politics Quarterly, 18*(4), 492.

Fox, Jonathan. (2001). Religious causes of international intervention in ethnic conflicts. *International Politics, 38*(4), 515-532.

Freytag, Andreas, Krüger, Jens J., Meierrieks, Daniel, & Schneider, Friedrich. (2011). The origins of terrorism: Cross-country estimates of socio-economic determinants of terrorism. *European Journal of Political Economy, 27, Supplement 1*(0), S5-S16.

Gadarian, Shana Kushner. (2010). The Politics of Threat: How Terrorism News Shapes Foreign Policy Attitudes. *Journal of Politics, 72*(2), 469-483.

Gakidou, Emmanuela, Cowling, Krycia, Lozano, Rafael, & Murray, Christopher JL. (2010). Increased educational attainment and its effect on child mortality in 175 countries between 1970 and 2009: a systematic analysis. *The Lancet, 376*(9745), 959-974.

Gleditsch, Nils Petter, Wallensteen, Peter, Eriksson, Mikael, Sollenberg, Margareta, & Strand, Havard. (2002). Armed Conflict 1946-2001: A New Dataset. *Journal of Peace Research, 39*(5), 615.

Goldstein, J.S. (2003). *War and gender: How gender shapes the war system and vice versa*: Cambridge University Press.

Gunawardena, Arjuna. (2006). Female black tigers: A different breed of cat? *Female suicide bombers: Dying for equality*, 81-90.

Gurr, Ted Robert. (1990). Terrorism in Democracies: Its Social and Political Bases. In W. Reich (Ed.), *Origins of Terrorism*. Cambridge, UK: Cambridge Univ. Press.

Gurr, Ted Robert. (1994). Peoples against states: Ethnopolitical conflict and the changing world system: 1994 presidential address. *International Studies Quarterly*, 347-377.

Hausmann, Ricardo, Tyson, Laura D., & Zahidi, Saadia. (2011). The Global Gender Gap Report 2011 Geneva, Switzerland: World Economic Forum.

Henderson, Errol A. (1997). Culture or Contiguity Ethnic Conflict, the Similarity of States, and the Onset of War, 1820-1989. *Journal of Conflict Resolution, 41*(5), 649-668.

Heston, Alan, Summers, Robert , & Aten, Bettina (2009). Penn World Table Version 6.3. from Center for International Comparisons of Production, Income and Prices at the University of Pennsylvania.

Hetherington, Marc, & Suhay, Elizabeth. (2011). Authoritarianism, Threat, and Americans' Support for the War on Terror. *American Journal of Political Science, 55*(3), 546-560. doi: 10.1111/j.1540-5907.2011.00514.x

Htun, Mala. (2003). *Sex and the State: Abortion, Divorce, and the Family under Latin American Dictatorships and Democracies*: Cambridge University Press

Hudson, Valerie M. (2012). *Sex and world peace*. New York: Columbia University Press.

Hudson, Valerie M., Caprioli, Mary, Ballif-Spanvill, Bonnie, McDermott, Rose, & Emmett, Chad F. (2008). The Heart of the Matter: The Security of Women and the Security of States. *International Security, 33*(3), 7-45.

Inglehart, Ronald, & Norris, Pippa. (2003). *Rising Tide: Gender Equality and Cultural Change Around the World*. Cambridge, UK. New York, USA.: Cambridge University Press.

Juergensmeyer, Mark. (2003). *Terror in the mind of God : the global rise of religious violence* (Third ed.). Berkley and Los Angeles: University of California Press.

Kabeer, Naila , & Stark, Agneta (Eds.). (2008). *Global perspectives on gender equality : Reversing the gaze*: Routledge.

Kabeer, Naila , Stark, Agneta, & Magnus, Edda. (2008). Introduction: Reversing the gaze. In N. Kabeer, A. Stark & E. Magnus (Eds.), *Global perspectives on gender equality : Reversing the gaze*
: Routledge.

Kaltenthaler, Karl, Miller, William J., Ceccoli, Stephen, & Gelleny, Ron. (2010). The Sources of Pakistani Attitudes toward Religiously Motivated Terrorism. *Studies in Conflict & Terrorism, 33*(9), 815-835. doi: 10.1080/1057610x.2010.501424

Kis-Katos, Krisztina, Liebert, Helge, & Schulze, Günther G. (2011). On the origin of domestic and international terrorism. *European Journal of Political Economy, 27*, S17-S36.

Klasen, Stephan. (2006). UNDP's Gender related Measures: Some Conceptual Problems and Possible Solutions. *Journal of Human Development, 7*(2), 243-274. doi: 10.1080/14649880600768595

Kouvo, Sari, & Levine, Corey. (2008). Calling a Spade a Spade: Tackling the 'Women and Peace' Orthodoxy. *Feminist Legal Studies, 16*(3), 363-367. doi: 10.1007/s10691-008-9102-5

Krieger, Tim, & Meierrieks, Daniel. (2011). What causes terrorism? *Public Choice, 147*(1), 3-27. doi: 10.1007/s11127-010-9601-1

Krueger, Alan B., & Male ková, Jitka (2003). Education, Poverty and Terrorism: Is There a Causal Connection? *The Journal of Economic Perspectives, 17*(4), 119-144. doi: 10.2307/3216934

LaFree, Gary, & Dugan, Laura. (2007). Introducing the Global Terrorism Database. *Terrorism & Political Violence, 19*(2), 181-204. doi: 10.1080/09546550701246817

Lai, Brian. (2007). 'Draining the Swamp': An Empirical Examination of the Production of International Terrorism, 1968-1998. *Conflict Management and Peace Science, 24*(4), 297-310. doi: http://cmp.sagepub.com/archive/

Laitin, David D. (1986). *Hegemony and Culture: Politics and Change among the Yoruba*: University of Chicago Press.

Li, Quan. (2005). Does Democracy Promote or Reduce Transnational Terrorist Incidents? *The Journal of Conflict Resolution, 49*(2), 278-297.

Li, Quan, & Schaub, Drew. (2004). Economic Globalization and Transnational Terrorism: A Pooled Time-Series Analysis. *The Journal of Conflict Resolution, 48*(2), 230-258.

Lichbach, Mark Irving. (1997). Social Theory and Comparative Politics. In M. I. Lichbach & A. S. Zuckerman (Eds.), *Comparative politics: Rationality, culture, and structure*: Cambridge University Press.

Long, J. Scott, & Freese, Jeremy (2006). *Regression Models for Categorical Dependent Variables Using Stata* (second ed.). College Station TX: Stata Press.

M'Cormack-Hale, Fredline Amaybel Olayinka, & M'Cormack-Hale, Fredline. (2012). *Gender, Peace and Security: Women's Advocacy and Conflict Resolution*: Commonwealth Secretarial.

MacFarquhar, Neil (2011, September 7, 2011). Peacekeepers' Sex Scandals Linger, On Screen and Off, *The New Yok Times*. Retrieved from http://www.nytimes.com/2011/09/08/world/08nations.html?pagewanted=all

Marshall, M. G. , & Jaggers, K. . (2002). Polity IV Project: Political Regime Characteristics and Transitions, 1800-2002: Dataset Users' Manual. from University of Maryland.

Mazrui, Ali Al'Amin. (1990). *Cultural forces in world politics*: J. Currey.

Melander, Erik. (2005). Gender Equality and Intrastate Armed Conflict. *International Studies Quarterly, 49*(4), 695-714.

Mickolus, Edward F. (1984). International Terrorism: Attributes of Terrorist Events, 1968-1977 [ITERATE 2]: Inter-university Consortium for Political and Social Research (ICPSR) [distributor]. Retrieved from http://dx.doi.org/10.3886/ICPSR07947.v1

Midlarsky, Manus I., Crenshaw, Martha, & Yoshida, Fumihiko. (1980). Why Violence Spreads: The Contagion of International Terrorism. *International Studies Quarterly, 24*(2), 262-298.

Newman, Edward. (2006). Exploring the "root causes" of terrorism. *Studies in Conflict & Terrorism, 29*(8), 749-772.

Nincic, Miroslav, & Nincic, Donna J. (2002). Race, gender, and war. *Journal of Peace Research, 39*(5), 547-568.

Norris, Pippa, & Inglehart, Ronald. (2001). Cultural Obstacles to Equal Representation. *Journal of Democracy, 12*(3), 126.

O'Rourke, Lindsey A. (2009). What's Special about Female Suicide Terrorism? *Security Studies, 18*(4), 681-718. doi: 10.1080/09636410903369084

Page, Benjamin I., & Shapiro, Robert Y. (1992). *The Rational Public: Fifty Years Of Trends In Americans*. Chicago, IL: University of Chicago Press. .

Pape, Robert. (2003). The Strategic Logic of Suicide Terrorism. *The American Political Science Review, 97*(3), 343-361.

Parashar, Swati. (2011). Gender, Jihad, and Jingoism : Women as Perpetrators, Planners, and Patrons of Militancy in Kashmir. *Studies in Conflict & Terrorism, 34*(4), 295-317. doi: 10.1080/1057610x.2011.551719

Piazza, James A. (2006). Rooted in Poverty?: Terrorism, Poor Economic Development, and Social Cleavages 1. *Terrorism & Political Violence, 18*(1), 159-177. doi: 10.1080/095465590944578

Piazza, James A. (2008). Incubators of Terror: Do Failed and Failing States Promote Transnational Terrorism? *International Studies Quarterly, 52*(3), 469-488.

Piazza, James A. (2011). Poverty, minority economic discrimination, and domestic terrorism. *Journal of Peace Research, 48*(3), 339-353. doi: 10.1177/0022343310397404

Piazza, James A., & Walsh, James Igoe. (2010). Physical integrity rights and terrorism. *Political Science and Politics, 43*(3), 411-414.

Ratcliffe, Rebekah (2011, December 8). Women in the military: around the world: The role of women in armed forces across the globe, *The Guardian*. Retrieved from http://www.guardian.co.uk/uk/2011/dec/08/women-in-military-around-world

Regan, Patrick M., & Paskeviciute, Aida. (2003). Women's Access to Politics and Peaceful States. *Journal of Peace Research, 40*(3), 287.

Robison, Kristopher K. (2010). Unpacking the Social Origins of Terrorism: The Role of Women's Empowerment in Reducing Terrorism. *Studies in Conflict & Terrorism, 33*(8), 735-756. doi: 10.1080/1057610x.2010.494171

Robison, Kristopher K., Crenshaw, Edward M., & Jenkins, J. Craig. (2006). Ideologies of Violence: The Social Origins of Islamist and Leftist Transnational Terrorism. *Social Forces, 84*(4), 2009-2026.

Ross, Marc Howard. (1997). Culture and Identity in Comparative Political Analysis. In M. I. Lichbach & A. S. Zuckerman (Eds.), *Comparative politics: Rationality, culture, and structure*: Cambridge University Press.

Ruddick, Sara. . (1989). *Maternal thinking: toward a politics of peace*: Beacon Press.

Sánchez-Cuenca, Ignacio, & de la Calle, Luis. (2009). Domestic Terrorism: The Hidden Side of Political Violence. *Annual Review of Political Science, 12*(1), 31-49.

Schmid, Alex. (2004). FRAMEWORKS FOR CONCEPTUALISING TERRORISM. *Terrorism and Political Violence, 16*(2), 197-221. doi: 10.1080/09546550490483134

Schweitzer, Yoram. (2006). *Female suicide bombers: dying for equality?* : Jaffee Center for Strategic Studies, Tel Aviv University.

Sjoberg, Laura. (2007). Agency, Militarized Femininity and Enemy Others: Observations From The War In Iraq. *International Feminist Journal of Politics, 9*(1), 82-101. doi: 10.1080/14616740601066408

Sjoberg, Laura, Cooke, Grace D., & Neal, Stacy R. (2011). Introduction: Women, Gender, and Terrorism In L. Sjoberg & C. E. Gentry (Eds.), *Women, Gender, and Terorism*. Athens and London: The University of Georgia Press.

Sjoberg, Laura, & Gentry, Caron E. (2007). *Mothers, monsters, whores : women's violence in global politics*

Smith, Tom W. (1984). The Polls: Gender and Attitudes Toward Violence. *Public Opinion Quarterly, 48*(1B), 384-396.

Speckhard, Anne. (2008). The Emergence of Female Suicide Terrorists. *Studies in Conflict & Terrorism, 31*(11), 1023-1051. doi: 10.1080/10576100802408121

Stern, Jessica. (2009). *Terror in the Name of God*: HarperCollins e-books.
Teorell, Jan, Nicholas Charron, Marcus Samanni, Sören Holmberg & Bo Rothstein. (2011). The Quality of Government Dataset. Retrieved January 12, 2012, from University of Gothenburg: The Quality of Government Institute http://www.qog.pol.gu.se
Tessler, Mark, & Warriner, Ina. (1997). Gender, feminism, and attitudes toward international conflict. *World Politics, 49*(2), 250.
Tickner, J. Ann. (1992). *Gender in international relations : feminist perspectives on achieving global security* New York Columbia University Press.
Togeby, Lise. (1994). The gender gap in foreign policy attitudes. *Journal of Peace Research, 31*(4), 375.
UN. (2004). *Women and peace and security: Report of the Secretary-General*. New York, NY: United Nations.
Urdal, Henrik. (2006). A clash of generations? Youth bulges and political violence. *International Studies Quarterly, 50*(3), 607-629.
Walsh, Denise (2011). *Women's Rights in Democratizing States: Just Debate and Gender Justice in the Public Sphere*. New York: Cambridge University Press.
WDR. (2012). World Development Report: Gender Equality and Development Washington D.C.: The World bank.
Weinberg, Leonard, & Eubank, William. (2011). Women's Involvement in Terrorism. *Gender Issues, 28*(1/2), 22-49. doi: 10.1007/s12147-011-9101-8
WfWi. (2008). 2008 Iraq Report: Amplifying the Voices of Women in Iraq *Stronger Women Stronger Nations*: Women for Women International.
WfWi. (2009). 2009 Afghanistan Report: Amplifying the Voices of Women in Afghanistan: Women for Women International.
WfWi. (2010). 2010 DRC Report: Amplifying the Voices of Women in Eastern Congo *Stronger Women Stronger Nations*: Women for Women International.
Wiedenhaefer, Robert M., Dastoor, Barbara Riederer, Balloun, Joseph, & Sosa-Fey, Josephine. (2007). Ethno-Psychological Characteristics and Terror-Producing Countries: Linking Uncertainty Avoidance to Terrorist Acts in the 1970s. *Studies in Conflict & Terrorism, 30*(9), 801-823. doi: 10.1080/10576100701514532
World Bank (2003). World Development Indicators 2003, Washington, DC: World Bank Office.
World Values Survey (2000). from World Values Survey Association

Chapter 4: Killing in the name of God: Religion and Lethality of Terrorist Attacks

4.1 Introduction

Not all societies face the same level of terrorism, and attacks are more deadly in some countries than others. In 76 countries between 1981 to 2004, a total of 4006 terror attacks took place, killing 6507 people. Out of these 4006 terror attacks, 202 attacks resulted in no fatalities, while 1869 attacks killed 5458 people (see Appendix 4-A). Also there are only seven countries where more than 100 people were killed in terror attacks in a year[1]. Why do some societies experience more violent and lethal terrorism than others? What factors determine the difference in lethal attacks suffered by one country and not the other?

A terrorist attack involves perpetrator, victim and audience. Focusing on terrorist organizations, studies show that organizational characteristics such as ideology, capability, organizational size and age, territorial control, connectedness / ties with other organizations and home-base country context that helps predict which organizations choose to kill (Asal & Rethemeyer, 2008a, 2008b). Although terrorism is a heavily contested term, it is generally understood as a political act of violence against state actors, so the appropriate level of analysis is state level factors (Hoffman, 2006). Empirical studies suggest certain country specific factors that influence target selection and existing

---

[1] The countries include Algeria, Columbia, South Africa, United States, India, Iraq and Turkey

empirical research has identified the role of democracy (Li, 2005), economic integration (Li & Schaub, 2004) and geographic neighborhoods of terrorism hot spots (Braithwaite & Li, 2007). Scholars agree that terrorism is not a random act of violence and terrorists are not irrational actors, in fact terrorism is calculated and orchestrated to deliver an ideological message to a specific audience by rationally acting terrorist organizations (Crenshaw, 1981; Hoffman, 2006; McCormick, 2003; Pape, 2003). Depending on the organizational ideology, the audience can be earthly, like governments, or supernatural holy entities. Scholars suggest strong connections between religion and rise of new terrorism (Hoffman, 1999; Juergensmeyer, 2003), yet so far study has empirically investigated the relationship between public attitudes towards religion and terrorism and the lack of research on the question is surprising given the recent surge in religiously motivated terrorism.

This study is a cross-national time series analysis of the impact of religious attitudes on the lethality of a terrorist attack, looking at 76 countries over the period 1981 to 2004 using Global Terrorism Database (GTD) and World Values Survey (WVS). The results suggest that more religious societies experience more lethal terror attacks, though I find that religiousness of a society has no impact on the number of terrorist incidents that a society experiences. The findings suggest that, ceteris paribus, religious attitudes of the society influence the lethality of an attack. This paper also explores the connections between Islamic fundamentalism and terrorism from an innovative perspective. Controlling for religious attitudes, this study examines whether societies with higher Muslim populations experience more lethal terrorism. The results show there is no significant relationship between Muslim populations and lethal terrorism. Overall this study provides empirical evidence that more religious societies are associated with more deadly attacks[2] and that there is no significant relationship between religious terrorism and Islam.

Research shows that religion and terrorism are connected in complex and perplexing ways, as demonstrated by the recent rise of religiously motivated terrorism (Fox & Sandler, 2004; Hoffman, 1995, 2006; Juergensmeyer, 2000, 2003). There is empirical evidence that terrorist organizations motivated by religious *and* ethno-nationalist ideologies are more lethal in their attacks than ethno-nationalist groups (Asal & Rethemeyer, 2008b). Actually religion is a double-edged sword that can be employed to propagate either peace or violence depending on the socio-economic and political context. Since no terrorist organization can operate without some kind of community or public support, human capital, social networks and material resources to carry out its attack, the religiousness of the society is a good indicator of the context in which terrorist organizations operate (Bagaji, Etila, Ogbadu, & Suie, 2012; Canetti, Hobfoll, Pedahzur, & Zaidise, 2010; Piazza, 2008b). Religious extremists are more successful at carrying out lethal attacks; hence we can safely assume that religious terrorist organizations find more sympathizers in religious societies than less religious ones.

---

[2] The Global Terrorism Database (GTD) does not provide any information about the perpetuator i.e. their demographics, identity, ideology or home base location (in case of transnational terrorism). It only records event-based information about the target country. So we are unable to analyze the direct causal relationship between religious societies and terrorist organizations carrying out lethal attacks in those societies. Also there is no global database about the identity of the victims, i.e. gender, nationality, ethnicity, religion, class or political views, which would help us examine which type of individuals are more vulnerable to terrorist attacks. Nevertheless GTD and the World Values Survey are the most comprehensive panel datasets available on terrorism and religious attitudes.

There are two main explanations as to why terrorist organizations carry out more lethal attacks in religious societies: the process of 'othering' and/or the use of mutual aid. Often religion acts as an identity marker between in-groups and out-groups in times of conflict, aggravating differences and hatred for 'other' or out-group members. Sacred texts in a religious society often provide a rhetoric of 'othering' which helps rationalize killing people belonging to a different religion, ethnicity or cultural tradition. Furthermore Juergensmeyer's (2003) work based on interviews of religious terrorists shows that often religious extremists and their supporters believe their audience is a higher spiritual authority and that killing more people is part of the apocalyptical supernatural cosmic war. Within religious societies, strong support networks and a body of radical supporters convinced about extremist ideology strengthen terrorist organization's capability, increase accessibility to the target and significantly lower the operational cost of carrying out a lethal attack (Hoffman & McCormick, 2004; McCormick, 2003).

In addition, there is evidence that religious extremist organizations in religious societies operate to provide social services through mutual aids (Berman, 2009). In absence of state providing social services to marginalized communities these organizations fill that service delivery gap. They advertise superiority of their ideological cause and gain support by providing social services, such as basic health facilities and education, food and water etc. Hence even though they kill more, they have a running list of new recruits from amongst their supporters and service beneficiaries. Religion might not be the only mobilizing force to rally support in favor of violence and terrorism, but it is a powerful trigger in circumstances where feelings of alienation, economic deprivation and political marginalization are simmering due to socio-economic or political discrimination based on religion or ethnicity (Oberschall, 2004; Satana et al., 2013).

The theoretical understanding of the connections between religion and terrorism is still rudimentary as there are very few empirical studies on this topic. Juergensmeyer's (2003) influential work on religion and terrorism unpacks these relationships employing a qualitative approach. A major contribution of this study is to help clarify the statistical relationship between religious attitudes and terrorism using a cross-sectional quantitative method. Furthermore, no previous study has used the same controls to examine religious attitudes and how they impact terrorism at a country level. For instance, Asal and Rethemeyer (2008b) focus on the terrorist organization level. This study is pioneering because it looks at country level predictors of terrorism in general and religiousness of a society in particular. In a similar study Capell and Sahliyeh (2007) examine the religious nature of the terrorist groups and lethality of their attacks, and find that religion does not explain lethality of an attack, though there are major flaws in their the research design[3]. Furthermore they limit their analysis to international attacks, whereas domestic terrorism is three to four times more prevalent than transnational terrorist events (Enders et al., 2011) and is also more violent (Sánchez-Cuenca & de la Calle, 2009).

---

[3] They employ ordinary least square regression to analyze number of people killed during 1980-2002. Their dependent variable is censored data with a natural lower limit of zero, which includes some countries experiencing high levels of lethality. Data from 1980-2004 based on Global Terrorism Database includes 3001 casualties in US in 2001, 1981 people killed in Peru in 1984 and in Rwanda 1558 people killed in 1994, which are all high casualty attacks, compared to many countries in the dataset, which have no attacks in that time period, or if there was a terror attack, nobody was killed. For such data, the appropriate estimation model is Tobit regression as the dependent variable is censored and maximum number of people killed for some countries is quite high.

The purpose of this study is to present an empirical analysis of the relationship between religion and terrorism from a global perspective, including both domestic and transnational attacks, using a suitable research design[4]. Given the long history and patterns of terrorism over time, there is tremendous research potential in analyzing the predictors of terrorism from a macro level (i.e. state level) of analysis to study patterns, causes, factors and driving forces behind terrorism in a broader fashion that might not be captured at the individual or organizational level.

This country-level analysis of religion and terrorism has important policy implications. A refined understanding of the dynamics of terrorism and its relationship to religious attitudes enables policy analysts to anticipate and estimate the size of future attacks at a country level. The results suggest that less religious societies are better protected against lethal terrorism, than strongly religious ones. Higher religious attitudes are strong predictors of number of people killed in a terror attack. This association between religious societies and lethal attacks indicates that religion can be employed to mobilize people for terrorist activities. Operating through mutual aids, religious extremists exploit the gap left by states of providing social service to marginalized communities, and use religion to mobilize support for terrorism. Therefore states must focus on provision of essential social services to all, regardless of religious, ethno-cultural, geographic or linguistic background in order to deter terrorism. Based on such empirical knowledge, policy makers and government can design effective counter

---

[4] Negative Binomial model for the number of terror attacks and Tobit estimation for number of people killed.

terrorism policies promoting values like religious tolerance, equality and freedom, social justice and inclusion; reversing the environment that encourages terrorist activities.

The paper is organized as follows. The first section reviews the literature on religion and terrorism and the resulting hypotheses. The second section lays out the research design, dependent and independent variables. The third section presents the estimation and the results. The final section interprets the results and concludes with the theoretical and policy implications of this study.

4.2 Links between Religion and Terrorism

The nature and characteristics of terrorism have changed over the years. Researchers studying terrorism identify 'old' and 'new' terrorism based on the changing trends in ideologies, motivations, tactics and strategies. Older forms of terrorism in the 1960s to 1980s were usually motivated by political left wing ideologies (e.g. Marxism) or ethno-nationalism and separatism (e.g. Irish or Palestinian movement) and were mostly secular in nature; seeking attention, publicity and authority (Bell, 1975; Copeland, 2001; Hoffman, 1999; Laquer, 1998; Pisano, 1989). Shortly after the World Trade Center bombing in 1993, that Kushner (1994) coined the term 'new terrorism'. Though there is no single inaugurating event that defines the transition into the new era of terrorism, scholars identify certain characteristics of this paradigm shift. In his influential work, Hoffman (1999) distinguishes a new era of terrorist violence, motivated by theological imperatives, which is bloodier and more destructive than the 'old terrorism'. He argues that the new breed of religious terrorism is more lethal than its secular counterparts, such as the left wing or ethnonationalist groups. The paradigm has shifted more to the right i.e.

terrorism engendered with religious fanaticism and a new set of values and worldview. The 'new' terrorism is more indiscriminate in killing, and it is increasingly more difficult to discern its motives (Juergensmeyer, 2003; Laquer, 1998). Nevertheless the simplistic compartmentalization of terrorism as 'old' and 'new' can be debated, given that terrorism has always been violent and religion has often been associated with violence (Copeland, 2001; Spencer, 2006)[5].

Aquaviva (1979) defines religion as a system of beliefs and practices related to an ultimate or supernatural being. It is a body of ideas and outlooks, which influences its believer's worldview, thoughts, opinions and actions (Haynes, 1998). There is long history of theorizing on state and religious organizations referred to as 'church state' relations in the literature, but this paper is interested in religion as a socio-political actor, with collective solidarity and group religiosity that seeks to accomplish a political change through violence.

Religion and terrorism are related in intricate ways as witnessed in events like the World Trade Bombing (1993), Tokyo subways gas attacks (1995), Oklahoma city bombing (1995), Omagh Northern Ireland bombing (1998), September 11 attacks (2001), Bali bombings (2002), London transit bombings (2005) along with the protracted history of suicide bombings and terrorist attacks in Israel and the Palestine Authority, Ireland, Egypt, Turkey, Russia, Chechnya, Kashmir, Algeria, Nigeria, Indonesia, and the ongoing bloodshed in Iraq[6], Pakistan[6] and Afghanistan[6] (Bagaji et al., 2012; Berman, 2009;

---

[5] Although this debate is critical it is outside the scope of this paper, the focus of which it to unpack the connection between the religious attitudes and terrorism in different societies.
[6] 'Iraq body count (IBC) has documented 112,017 - 122,438 civilian deaths from violence between 20 March 2003 and 14 March 2013'. See http://www.iraqbodycount.org/ (Retrieved June 15, 2013)

Bloom, 2005; Fox & Sandler, 2004; Hoffman, 2006; Juergensmeyer, 2001). The lethal combination of terrorism and religious fundamentalism is not restricted to one religious tradition as Christians, Muslims, Hindus, Sikhs and Buddhists all have actively engaged in killing people in the name of God/ or a Holy Entity (Emerson & Hartman, 2006; Fox, 2002; Juergensmeyer, 2003; Tambiah, 1992). It can be argued that even secular terrorist groups tend to operate like religious ones, for they operate like sects with religious fervor and affinity. For example the Liberation Tigers of Tamil Eelam (LTTE) and Kurdish PKK (Parti Karkerani Kurdistan) leaders were revered as God-like figures with unquestioned authority over followers (Radu, 2003).

4.2.1 Use of 'othering' in Religious Terrorism

The literature on political violence informs us that extremists employ the concept of 'othering' to justify and sanctify killing. The concept of 'othering' encompasses the process of differentiating an individual or group on the basis of religion, sect, ethnicity, political ideology, language or culture, as having lesser ethical or moral status than the members of the terrorist group. They are marked as 'other' because they reject a widely accepted moral or spiritual position (Juergensmeyer, 2003). Although there is no single meaning or settled interpretation of otherness, it implies an implicit judgment and a process of exclusion and inclusion, of attributing power to some and powerlessness of

---

[7] More than 24,000 people both civilians and troops were killed in terrorist attacks during the period between 2001 and 2008. Another 25,000 plus people died during military offensives against Taliban insurgents in the restive tribal regions since 2008.' See http://tribune.com.pk/story/527016/pakistani-victims-war-on-terror-toll-put-at-49000/
8 'the UN Assistance Mission in Afghanistan (UNAMA) recording 1,462 conflict-related civilian deaths in the first six months of the year (2013), a 15 percent increase since 2010' see
http://www.hrw.org/world-report-2012/world-report-2012-afghanistan

others[9]. 'Othering' is actively employed both by religious and non-religious terrorist groups. It implies unfamiliarity, disapproval, difference or distance of self from the enemy. It takes its shape and interpretation based on the cultural context where it is operationalized, yet it functions in similar ways in different settings i.e. of creating an emotional distance between self and other, rendering killing of other justifiable and part of the organizational goal.

In the context of studies on conflict and religion, research shows that 'othering' is employed to create a cultural distance between 'we' and 'others', and this binary code is a symbolic marker of who to trust or distrust (Terren, 2010). Religion is a powerful cultural marker in conflict because it provides group identity and generates in-group and out-group polarization (Kunovich & Hodson, 1999; Seul, 1999; Wellman & Tokuno, 2004). Wellman and Tokuno (2004) state, "...tension and conflict are inherent in all religious groups and are central to their identity formation and group mobilization. Once again, violence is not often a religion's intent, but as an outcome of its relation to culture and politics, it is certainly not an uncommon consequence" (p293). Extremist groups often employ narratives of otherness during conflict and political violence (Mayaram, 1993) and social and cultural separation based on sacred/theological texts makes terrorist attacks profoundly vicious and deadly. Extremists can manipulate religious symbols and texts to invoke religious sentiments of supporters, give religious interpretations to their

---

[9] The epistemology of 'otherness' can be traced to sociological, cultural studies and anthropological discourses for understanding construction of identity and social differences. Said (1979) theorized the superiority complex of the West, which belittled anything non-European as other, inferior and savage. Over the years this duality has been used for different groups of people, like woman defined as other of man (De Beauvoir, 1997; Irigaray & Guynn, 1995), black as other of white (Fanon, 1967) and Jew as other of Gentile (Sartre, 1965).

sense of alienation /isolation, legitimize use of violence and justify elimination of the group defined as their enemy[10]. Even though religion is not inherently violent, combined with other factors, like political marginalization, economic grievances and ethno-cultural differences, it has the potential to add fuel to fire. It played a significant role in intensifying ethno-nationalist conflicts, as seen in Sri-Lanka[11], Bosnia, Northern Ireland, Sudan, Uganda, Kashmir and Former Yugoslavia, where the other side was depicted as demonic and satanic (Kunovich & Hodson, 1999; Little, 2005; Powers, 1996; Schäfer, 2004). In all these instances, othering is employed to justify killing perceived enemies. Depending on the goal, ideology and world-view of the terrorist group, the 'other' can be an individual, a group of people, or state governments at the local, national or global level.

With the strong association between violence and religion, it appears to be easier for radical organizations to employ 'othering' rhetoric in more religious societies. Furthermore it implies that certain sections of religious societies are more responsive and sympathetic to religious extremists who believe in killing for their cause. Religious societies tend to be more divided on the issue of moral superiority, considering adherents of their religious tradition closer to salvation and truth than non-adherents (Wellman & Tokuno, 2004). Competing for superiority over each other, the divide can be between religions, like Al-Qaeda and its Islamic associates waging holy war i.e. *jihad* against a Christian US and Jewish Israel, Palestinian Islamic organizations attacking Jewish state

---

[10] All suicide bombers in the study by Berrebi (2003) thought they were serving a higher purpose by killing their enemy.
[11] See Liyanage, Priyath (2002, 31 October). Sri Lanka's 'Muslim question' BBC, available at http://news.bbc.co.uk/2/hi/south_asia/2381015.stm

of Israel, Hindu-Muslim communal riots in India, LTTE attacks against state representatives for Buddhist Sinhalese discrimination of Hindu-Tamil community. The rhetoric of otherness is also deployed between sects to justify killing and violence, such as the Catholic Protestant divide in the Northern Ireland; bloodshed between Shias/ Sunnis in Iraq and Pakistan and other Muslim countries; radical Tehrik-e-Taliban Pakistan (TTP) trying to impose sharia law in Pakistan and attacking military, law enforcement and civilians for not following 'true' Islam and Christian fundamentalists in the US attacking abortion clinics on theological grounds.

Terrorists attack people or property to pressure their audience. Depending on their goals, ideology, audience and capability, they attack state actors like the military[12] and law enforcement agencies, political actors or civilians. Terrorism is a public act of violence, or threat of violence, with political motives to provoke a sense of fear in an audience, so much so that Jenkins equates terrorism with a 'theatre' [13] and Juergensmeyer views it as 'performance violence' loaded with symbolic meaning (Crenshaw, 1981; Hoffman, 1999; Juergensmeyer, 2003). Scholars theorize that one of the most significant differences between secular and religious terrorism is the choice of audience. Scholars suggest that religious terrorism may be more deadly because its adherents invoke a supernatural audience through religious ideologies, while leftist, anarchist and ethno

---

[12] For instance Hizbollah attack on marine barrack in Beirut 1983, LTTE targeting Sri Lankan law enforcement agencies, Taliban and Tehrik-i-Taliban Pakistan continuous attack on military personal in Pakistan for assisting US war on terror in Afghanistan

[13] Hoffman, 'Inside Terrorism', p. 132, quotes from Brian Jenkins, "International Terrorism: A New Mode of Conflict," in David Carlton and Carlo Schaerf, eds., International Terrorism and World Security (London: Croom Helm, 1975).

nationalists are staging acts for earthly audience[] (Asal & Rethemeyer, 2008b; Gressang IV, 2001; Hoffman, 1995; Rapoport, 1984; Tilly, 2003). Terrorist groups with religious ambitions are not appeased with mere territorial or earthly compensations[], because they tend to view their struggle like a cosmic war between good and evil, of epic proportions, promising heavenly rewards for the victor (Juergensmeyer, 2003; Laqueur, 2004). The enemy is demonized and dehumanized to a level that killing the 'other' is seen as destroying evil[], and the death of the perpetuator /suicide bomber is celebrated as martyrdom[17].

Research shows that terrorism is a political act with social origins and roots, and the socio-cultural and political context has an influence on the levels and intensity of terrorism a country experiences (Canetti et al., 2010; Crenshaw, 1981; Robison, 2010; Robison et al., 2006; Turk, 2004; Ziemke, 2009). Terren (2010) argues that any social action takes place within a context of preexisting frame of meaning. This indicates that

---

[14] Hoffman explains that, 'For the religious terrorist, violence is a sacramental act or divine duty, executed in direct response to some theological demand or imperative and justified by scripture. Religion therefore functions as a legitimizing force, specifically sanctioning wide-scale violence against an almost open-ended category of opponents'(1999, VII).

[15] Religious extremists and terrorist do make territorial demands and other concessions, like prisoner swaps, money for hostages and safe passage etc, but these short run demands are part of their long-term objectives and goals to annihilate the enemy, and to establish their own authority. 'What makes religious violence particularly savage and relentless is that its perpetrators have placed such religious images of divine struggle- cosmic war- in service of worldly political battles'(Juergensmeyer, 2000)(p146).

[16] Juergensmeyer (2003) calls this process 'satanization' of the enemies i.e. reducing their legitimacy and justifying their destruction. The process entails creating satanic enemies / opponent, and when they reject ones moral or spiritual position, it becomes imperative to delegitimize, humiliate and destroy them to assert ones moral power over them. This dehumanization allows for massive atrocities and justifies acts of terrorism. Dehumanizing the enemy as subhuman or unworthy of living justifies their bloodshed for a greater cause that transcends earthly rewards.

[17] Radical religious organizations have developed the cult of martyrdom, which glorifies sacrifices and celebrates suicide bombers in their media campaigns, to inspire new recruits. They also provide generous financial rewards for martyrs and their families. It is reported that Saddam Hussein's Baathist party awarded $10,000-25,000 per martyr in the Palestinian territory (see "Palestinian gets Saddam funds," BBC News, March 13 2003).

attitudes of religiousness influence terrorist's decision to kill more people within a particular socio-cultural context. It also implies that it is a lot easier for religious extremists to appeal for public support using rhetoric of 'other' in religious societies than in less religious ones.

Religious radicals are particularly lethal terrorists because they carry out high casualty attacks[18]. Religiously inspired terrorists are willing to kill and be killed for spiritual convictions. They see themselves as above and opposed to secular laws and values therefore, for them, everybody is a legitimate target (Cronin, 2003). Al-Qaeda and its associates are the best example of groups that attack soft targets and kill indiscriminately.

Religious terrorists' decision to kill is based on their religious ideologies, the cultural context, sociopolitical settings and their worldviews (Berrebi, 2003). Their values and cultural influences play an important role in terrorism, and religious terrorism is linked to the religious understandings, trends and patterns within a particular society. For example family background, connections and consent are important elements in individual's decision to join religious militant groups. Focusing on Hezbollah in Lebanon, Schbley (2003) found that community and family connections are integral for encouraging recruitment, another study found that Palestinian militants in Lebanon had family support for their activities (Post, Sprinzak, & Denny, 2003); Orbach (2004) states

---

[18] Analyzing data retrieved from US State Department, from 1968 to 2007, Berman (2009) finds that secular terrorist organizations committed 2077 attacks, killing 2668 persons, with an average of 1.3 causalities per attack, while religious organizations killed 6706 people in 1852 attacks, with an average of 3.6 causalities per attack. Including 9/11 attacks raises the fatalities to 9,689 and average lethality to 5.2. On the list of these twenty religious organizations, eighteen are Islamic.

that families are central to Islamic militancy[19]; and Abou Zahab (2008) found family's, especially mother's, consent to be crucial for Lashkar-e-Taiba's recruitment.

Of course not all organizations choose to kill, and studies suggest that non-lethal terrorist organizations are either not ideologically driven to kill, or lack the capability to do so (Asal & Rethemeyer, 2008a). The capability of the organization to kill includes elements like human capital and social connections, financial resources, technical expertise and access to restricted places and material (Benmelech & Berrebi, 2007). Both ideology and capability makes religious organizations more lethal than others and motivates deliberately exaggerated violence. Capability is strongly dependent on the community and social setup in which these organizations operate. Terrorist attacks usually involve community support, and in many cases, a large organizational network, making it a collective decision with an ideological and moral backing (Juergensmeyer, 2000). Recent research suggests that better-connected terrorist groups are more successful at killing people, as terrorist networks enhance the capability of groups to share resources, training, skills and techniques (Asal & Rethemeyer, 2006).

4.2.2. Mutual Aid and Lethality

One reason for popular support for some religious terrorist organizations is that they fill an important gap left by the state by providing essential social services.

---

[19] "Following are the words of the mother of the shahid Muhammad Farhat: ''Jihad is a commandment imposed upon us. We must instill this idea in our son's souls all the time . . . and this is what encouraged me to sacrifice Muhammad in Jihad for the sake of Allah. Because I love my son, I encouraged him to die a martyr's death for the sake of Allah. I sacrificed Muhammad as part of my obligation...This is an easy thing...I, as a mother, naturally encouraged the love of Jihad in the soul of Muhammad and in the souls of all my sons . . . (I) asked Allah to make his operation successful and give him the martyrdom . . . After the martyrdom (operation), my heart was peaceful about Muhammad'' (Al-Sharq Al-Awsat, London, June 5, 2002). Taken from Orbach (2004) p121.

Regardless of religious denomination, radical terrorist groups are providers of essential social services through mutual aid, whereby individual members support the community through charity (Berman, 2009). Berman builds his notion of mutual aid on Iannaccone's framework of 'club' model[20]. Like 'club' members, many willingly adhere to social norms, sacrifices and prohibitions within radical religious communities in order to benefit from the social services provision and mutual aid (Iannaccone & Berman, 2006). This further defines the difference between members and non-members, excluding the nonmembers and reinforcing the process of 'othering'.

The notion of mutual aid helps to explain the community support that radical religious organizations continue to evoke, in spite of their massive carnage. Sketching hopes of a better future and overstating their goals inspires new recruits for religious radicals. Be it Hezbollah, Hamas, Lashkar-i-Tayyabia (LT)[21], Muslim Brotherhood or Al Qaeda, terrorist organizations thrive on generous charity networks. Religious organizations promise religious schools, basic medical treatment, a meager financial support and support communities with social services that the state has failed to provide (Haq, 2008). Relative deprivation theory posits grievance as a reason for eruption of political violence to redress political grievances and economic inequalities (Gurr, 1970). In his regard Urdal (2006) finds evidence that youth bulge, institutional bottlenecks, lack of political representation and openness, economic constraints and crowding in urban

---

[20] Iannaccone, Laurence R. "Sacrifice and stigma: reducing free-riding in cults, communes, and other collectives." Journal of political economy (1992): 271-291.

[21] National counterterrorism center records that Lashkar-i-Tayyabia coordinated extensive humanitarian relief and charitable activates for the October 2005 earthquake victims in Kashmir, and also during the floods in Punjab in 2010. It operates through its front organization, Jamaat-ud-Dawa. See http://www.nctc.gov/site/groups/let.html

centers increases the risks of political violence. It is these conditions that are advantageous for religious recruitment. Reversing these conditions has the potential to reverse the rise in terrorism, as studies show that higher social welfare spending in fields of education, health and unemployment benefits significantly reduces terrorism (Azam & Thelen, 2008; Burgoon, 2006; Krieger & Meierrieks, 2010).

There is no consensus in the literature about direct effects of aggregate economic condition on terrorism (Berrebi, 2003; Krueger & Male ková, 2003; Krueger & Laitin, 2008; Krueger & Male ková, 2003; Li & Schaub, 2004; Piazza, 2006; Shapiro & Fair, 2009). Even though poverty per se does not cause terrorism, when combined with other factors like deprivation, marginalization, hopelessness, resentment, economic and political grievances, it provides a pretext for extremists to penetrate deeper into the community and manipulate the feelings of exclusion and humiliation to perpetuate violence (Newman, 2006; Oberschall, 2004). Research shows that when excluded from government, extremist factions within ethnic minorities employ religious ideology as a mobilizing force for violent action (Satana et al., 2013). This suggests that public support for radical religious organizations is linked to the social services they provide and also to the religious ideology that they advertise[22].

4.2.3 Suicide Terrorism and Lethality

But why do terrorist organizations decide to kill people to forward their cause? Scholars suggest that killing more has greater payoffs, generates wider publicity,

---

[22] Looking at the Pakistani society, Fair, Malhotra, and Shapiro (2012) find that even though religious practice is not related to support of militant groups, people who believe in jihad show more support for violent groups. Jihad is the Islamic concept of waging war /struggle against 'non-believers.

augments organizational profile, boosts recruitment and resource generation, propels the cause and gains prompt government attention and concessions (Asal & Rethemeyer, 2008b; Gould & Klor, 2010; McCormick, 2003). Higher causalities induce greater publicity, and out of all the tactics to kill indiscriminately, terrorists have learnt that suicide bombing is the most efficient tactic to maximize lethality of an attack[23] (Hoffman, 2006; Pape, 2003; Schweitzer, 2000).

From a counter terrorism perspective, the organizational modus operandi and other socio-political conditions provide valuable information for efforts to control the surge of terrorism. Studies show that there is no single generic profile of a suicide bomber (Merari, 2004; Speckhard, 2008; Sprinzak, 2000) nevertheless focusing on the political and organizational features of terrorists can help cut off the supply side of suicide terrorism (Piazza, 2008b). Likewise Sprinzak argues that even if individuals are willing to die, it is the recruiters that indoctrinate would-be bombers with a sense or purpose and a heavenly reward to carry out an attack. Similarly Pape (2003) points out the two edged effect of suicide terrorism, which aims to kill the largest number of people, but can result in loss of support amongst moderate segments of the community at the same time as it attracts support of radical elements.

Interestingly, scholars studying suicide terrorism find that left wing or ethno-nationalist terrorism can be as indiscriminately violent as religiously motivated terrorists (Bloom, 2005; Bloom, 2003; Pape, 2003, 2005). Likewise Pape (2003) finds little

---

[23] Suicide bombing is the most efficient and highly lethal terrorism strategy, originally initiated by Hezbollah and the Liberation Tigers of Tamil Eelam (LTTE) and rapidly adopted by religious radicals. Since its inception, it has risen at an alarming rate, from 3 suicide attacks per year in 1980's to 25 per year in 2001 (see Berman (2009))

evidence of connection between suicide bombing and Islamic fundamentalism and concludes that suicide bombing in fact transcends ethnic, religious and political boundaries[24]. It appears that religion, although a powerful persuasion, is neither a necessary nor sufficient condition for suicide bombing (Merari, 2004).

4.2.4 Islamic Fundamentalism and Lethality

Since 9/11, heightened attention has been paid to Islamic fundamentalism. Al-Qaeda and its associates have adopted suicide terrorism as their signature tactic to kill maximum number of people. Very often, Islamic fundamentalism is seen as synonymous with religious terrorism, especially suicide bombing. Studies show that Islamic movements were responsible for 81% of all suicide attacks since 9/11 (Hoffman 2006). In this respect Bar (2004) contends that Islamic radicals portray a dichotomous worldview of *Dar-al-Islam* (The house of Islam) and *Dar-al-Harb* (The house of war), where every individual Muslim is obligated to wage jihad to evict an 'infidel' occupier from a Muslim country (e.g. Kashmir, Afghanistan, Chechnya and Palestine). Bar further argues that Islamic radicals see the solution in re-Islamization of Muslim societies including Islamic rebellion against 'apostate' and 'western influenced' governments and Muslim populations for forsaking true Islamic teaching (e.g. Islamic movements in Iran, Egypt, Saudi Arabia and Pakistan). The centrality of the duty for Jihad is stretched to Muslims residing in foreign lands with the promulgation of *Fatwas*[25], justifying violence and

---

[24] LTTE carried out 168 suicide attacks between 1987- 2000 and Kurdish PKK and Al-Aqsa Martyrs Brigades, both nationalist groups, have actively conducted suicide bombings. See Yoram Schweitzer, "Suicide Terrorism: Development and Characteristics", International Policy Institute for Counter Terrorism, (21 April 2000), available at: www.ict.org.il/articles/articledet.cfm? articleid=112

[25] Islamic analysis and ruling by authoritative scholar

terrorism in pursuit of Islamic goals and to pressurize 'infidels' to exit Muslim homelands.

Given the popular association of Islamic fundamentalism and violent terrorism, it is often assumed that higher Muslim population in a country is an indication of presence of radical religious groups who choose to carry out lethal attacks. This assumption has not been tested within the context of religiousness attitudes and terrorism. No previous study has looked at the percentage of Muslim population in a country and whether it is connected with lethality of an attack. This paper tests this assumption, to check whether societies with a higher Muslim population are in any way associated with lethality of an attack.

4.2.5 Rise in Religious Terrorism

The global rise of religious terrorism necessitates a cross-national analysis of its prevalence and patterns. Even though religiousness varies by religious tradition and socio-cultural context, religious violence has increased over the years. Religious violence exhibits similar patterns due to increased globalization and advancements in communication technology[26]. Globalization facilitates religious affinities to connect beyond national borders and geographical regions (Juergensmeyer, 2003). Furthermore religious terrorists are proficient and active users of Internet and cutting edge technology to share expertise, build connections, advertise their cause and hire new recruits (Weimann, 2011).

---

[26] Rapoport argues that 'sacred terror' has similar characteristics, regardless of how different the religions are from each other. (See David C. Rapoport, "Fear and Trembling: Terrorism in Three Religious Traditions," American Political Science Review 78 (1984): 668–672)

Some scholars view this recent rise of religious violence as a reaction to forces of modernization and refer to it as the 'return to religion'. This return to religion is especially true in the developing countries, where modernization is equated to secularization and seen as a threat that undermines traditional value systems. In fact the return or reemergence of modern religious movements is viewed as a response to the failure and disappointment with modernization, which is viewed as the culprit for increase in inequities and social injustice (Haynes, 1998; Juergensmeyer, 2003). This connection between modernization and social injustice provides room to religious fundamentalists to gather public support by offering social services and propagating religious extremism. Additionally the modern secular nationalism is by its nature opposed to role of religion in public life. Haynes (1998) argues that this crisis of religion combined with fear of modernization acts as a bugle call for radical religionists and their supporters.

Religion is indeed a potent force for social and political change, and given situations of economic grievances or political marginalization, religious organizations use a variety of tactics and strategies ranging from endorsing religious right parties to violence and terrorism to achieve their goals. Terrorism is regarded a weapon of the weak and religion bolsters support for violent means to restore order and harmony according to religious world-view of the organized religions.

Not all religiosity is negative and we cannot ignore the positive force of religion for progressive social change. There is profound contribution of religion to peace activism and peace-building e.g. role of the church in the Civil Rights Movement in the US, in the social justice movement in many countries in Latin America, peace activism during Vietnam war, in conflicts like Kashmir, Israel/Palestine, Iraq, Sudan, Macedonia and Nigeria (Henry, 2010; Smock et al., 2009).

The dichotomy is that 'Religion kills. Religion brings peace' (p 291) (Wellman & Tokuno, 2004). The symbolic boundaries and belief systems of religion mobilize individuals to form group identities, which sometimes leads to violence within or between groups. Religion and violence seem to be tied in a mutual bond of need especially when some believers accept the divine mandate for violence with unquestioned certainty (Juergensmeyer, 2003; Wellman & Tokuno, 2004). Societies develop cultures of violence, and religion provides a potent sanctification for killing for a divine cause. It is possible that many of these extremists groups might not be religious per se, but religious connections provide significant network opportunities. It is for this reason that religious conflict and violence can easily surpass national borders and operate in a global manner (Fox, 2001a, 2004).

Hypotheses:

The above discussion shows that religion and terrorism are linked in complex and intricate ways. Like other domestic state level factors that affect terrorism, attitudes towards religion is also an important facet that would affect terrorism. The theoretical links between religion and terrorism are based on the concept of 'othering' and religion providing identity markers for in-group and out-group, whereby killing members of out-group is morally justified for a greater cause. Religious groups also provide social services to build public support. We would expect more religious organizations to find more support in religious societies and therefore it is easier to carry out deadly attacks against out-group or 'other'. Further this study empirically tests the popular assumption of Muslim population being more active in religious violence. This discussion leads to the following hypotheses:

H1: Holding all else constant: Religious societies experience higher number of terrorist attacks.

H2: Religious societies are more likely to experience higher number of fatalities in terrorist attacks.

H3: Controlling for religiousness, societies with higher percentage of Muslims is associated with more lethal terrorism.

4.3 Research Design

To test the hypotheses this study employs a cross-national time-series analysis of religiousness of a society and its impact on the incidents and lethality of terrorism for 76 countries, over 1981-2004 for which full temporal data is available.

Dependent Variable:

For this study two dependent variables are employed, the incidents of terrorism and the lethality of a terror attack. The data is collected from Global Terrorism Database (GTD) an open-source and publically available database for more than 200 countries and disputed territories, from 1970-2010 (LaFree & Dugan, 2007). It is the aggregated number of domestic and international terrorist attacks and number of people killed as a result of those attacks, in a country in a single year. As the data is drawn from GTD, therefore this study employs the definitional criteria set by GTD[27]. Although it is a

---

[27] GTD criteria for recording an event as a terrorist event includes that the event has to be intentional, be violent or entail threat of it, carried out by non-state actors outside the realm of legitimate warfare. Also

widely used data set, GTD has certain inherent limitations since it is based on newspaper sources and this may introduce bias due to underreporting. Presently this is the most comprehensive data available on terrorism that includes both domestic and international attacks[28].

Independent Variable- Religiousness:

Data on attitude towards religion is drawn from the World Values Survey (WVS) dataset. The WVS data is based on cross-national and longitudinal survey research programs carried out in 97 societies around the world, over a period of six waves i.e. 1981-1984, 1989-1993, 1994-1999, 1999-2004, 2005-2006, and 2008-2010[29] (the list of sample size for each wave is available at Appendix 4-B). The World Values Survey includes a wide range of societies at different levels of modernization based on the categorization of Human Development Index (HDI)[30] produced annually by United Nations Development Program. Due to coverage of all variables of interest in the model, the number of countries included in this study is 76 over a period of 1981-2004. The list of included countries is available at Appendix 4-C.

Religiousness of a society data is based on the World Values Survey question 'How important is God in your life?' The response interval scale ranges from 1 to 10,

---

one of the two conditions must be fulfilled that the attack is carried out to influence a group larger than the immediate target and/ or the attack has a political, social, religious or ideological goal.

[28] For this study separating domestic and transnational terror attacks is not feasible as the number of observation would be less than 100 and it does not allow for a meaningful analysis. Also a recent study shows that domestic and transnational terrorism are driven by similar forces (Kis-Katos et al., 2011). Another data limitation is with regard to type /kind of attack. GTD data is in country-year format, so we cannot analyze the kind/type of attack, whether it is a suicide attack, car bomb or any other mean of destruction.

[29] No world values survey data is available for the years 1985 to 88.

[30] The Human Development Index (HDI) is a ranking of countries based on composite data on life expectancy, educational attainment and income, produced annually by United Nations Development Program (UNDP). For further information please see http://hdr.undp.org/en/statistics/hdi/

where 1 means 'very important' and 10 means 'not at all important'. It also means that 1 means highly religious and 10 means less religious societies. The surveys are based on random probability samples and all interviews are conducted face-to face. The individual level World Values Survey data is aggregated to the country-year format. The value of each observation is the country mean for the variable.

There is a wide range of religious traditions around the world, but this study is focused on the general attitude of religiousness, of belief and importance of God in one's life, regardless of religious tradition. A religious society does not necessarily mean it has a religious government as well, because many countries with secular constitutional arrangement are highly religious societies. For instance on the world values survey religiousness scale of 0 to 10, US is 2.73, Turkey is 1.94 and India is 2.87, which depict strong religious values. Societies consist of a wide range and varying degrees of religious communities and so it is unrealistic to have a dichotomous category of religious or secular society. Hence the aggregated values of individual responses regarding religion provide robust and reliable information about the level of religious values in a society (See Appendix 4-D for a list of 10 most and least religious societies and their religiousness score).

Another variable of interest is the religiosity scale, which is aggregated individual-level data in country-year format based on World Values Survey data and drawn from Inglehart and Norris (2003). The values are country mean of individual responses for that year. It is a 0-100 scale composed of six survey questions, where 0 means less religiosity and 100 is high religiosity score (see Appendix 4-E for the survey questions). Both the religion variables are highly correlated so they are not included in the same models. Other variables were also considered for inclusion in the model. Religiousness is often associated with levels of tolerance in a society. World Values Survey has data on tolerance levels in a society but it has numerous inconsistencies in reported responses between waves. Therefore this variable was not employed given its unreliable information.

To test for the impact of Muslim population and levels of lethality, data is taken from LaPorta, Lopez-de-Silane, Pop-Eleches, and Shleifer (2004), which gives a percentage of Muslim population in a country in that year.

Independent Variables- Controls:

Review of seminal research on determinants of terrorism suggests variables that must be used to control for various state characteristics that impact terrorism. Terrorism literature strongly suggests that state factors like political regime, population size, gross domestic product (GDP) per capita, past conflicts that a country was involved in and whether it experienced past terror attacks influence the terrorism a country experiences (Abadie, 2006; Blomberg, Hess, & Weerapana, 2004; Braithwaite & Li, 2007; Enders & Sandler, 2005; Eubank & Weinberg, 1994, 2001; Li, 2005; Li & Schaub, 2004; Midlarsky et al., 1980; Piazza, 2006, 2008a). For economic variable the log for real GDP per capita is included (Abadie, 2006).

Data on control variables are drawn from the Quality of Government database which is a rich source of cross-national and time series comparative data (Teorell, 2011). The data for polity i.e. form of government is based on Marshall and Jaggers (2002). It is a scale of level of democracy ranging from zero i.e. least democratic to ten for most democratic. Population size and real GDP per capita is taken from Heston et al. (2009).

The data about involvement in past incidents is based on UCDP/PRIO Armed conflict dataset, which is a count of the inter-state and intra-state conflicts a country experienced in a year (Gleditsch et al., 2002). For the variable on past terror attacks, the incidents of terrorism are lagged by one year.

Two other control variables are included in the regression models, region and year fixed effects. The year fixed effects account for trends in terrorism and region fixed effects controls for variation in terrorism in different regions, depending on levels of deterrence, imposing greater costs on terrorists, contagion effect or preference for a certain target country (Braithwaite & Li, 2007; Lai, 2007a; Midlarsky et al., 1980). GTD keeps a track of the location of each attack by country and region, and has coded 13 different regions based on geography and culture[31].

4.4 Estimation

The unit of analysis is a single country in a single year. The first dependent variable is the number of terrorist incidents that a country experiences in a single year. Given the nature of the dependent variable as count data an ordinary least square model (OLS) is not the correct specification, so a count model is recommended. Since the variance for incidents of terrorism is bigger than its mean, a Poisson model cannot be employed (Long & Freese, 2006) (see Table-4.1 for descriptive statistics for the variables). There are a number of country-year observations with no terror attacks i.e. an

---

[31] GTD divides regions into 13 categories, where 1= North America, 2= Central America & Caribbean, 3= South America, 4= East Asia, 5= Southeast Asia, 6= South Asia, 7= Central Asia, 8= Western Europe, 9= Eastern Europe, 10= Middle East & North Africa, 11= Sub-Saharan Africa, 12= Russia & the Newly Independent States (NIS), 13= Australasia & Oceania.

over dispersion of zeros, and the data is skewed to the right. Overdispersion leads to underestimated standard errors. We can either use a standard negative binomial regression model or a zero-inflated negative binomial (ZINB) model as both allow for overdispersion[32]. In past studies, negative binomial model is mostly used to estimate count of terror attacks for country-year data (Li, 2005; Li & Schaub, 2004; Piazza & Walsh, 2010; Robison, 2010). However for robustness check, ZINB regression is calculated but the model does not converge, thus negative binomial estimation is preferred for the analysis. In the negative binomial models robust standard errors are calculated to cope with heteroskedasticity, and clustered by country to control for country specific variations (Williams, 2000).

Given the nature of the second dependent variable (i.e. the number of people killed in an attack) the most appropriate estimation technique is Tobit because the data is constrained by natural endpoint. The number of people killed has technically no upper limit but it has a natural lower limit at zero. A classic case for using Tobit model is that we do not know the exact reason for the natural limit. Likewise if nobody is killed it could be due to a number of reasons, for instance by design (organization had no intention to kill) or due to a technical error (bomb did not go off).

This study uses panel data which has inherent strengths as it allows for more accurate predictions about dynamics of change, than time series or cross national data alone (Hsiao, 2003). It also helps to construct and test complicated behavioral models, which are not possible otherwise. However, like any other quantitative research on

---

[32] Some scholars believe the difference in fit between negative binomial regression model and zero-inflated negative binomial model is usually trivial. (See Paul Allison, August 7,2012 http://www.statisticalhorizons.com/zero-inflated-models)

terrorism, this study has certain data and temporal constrains given its cross sectional design and span of over twenty years. A large panel data, drawn from various sources runs the risk of missing data. Such problems occurred with the terrorism data. For the number of people killed in an attack, a number of observations are unknown. Dropping these values is not advisable because for a particular country, that terror attack might be the only one for a particular year. I use imputed data for number of people killed drawn from Deloughery (2009) where missing values for number killed is generated using a Tobit model and the number killed is a function of the year, country and type of attack.

Although the World Values Survey (WVS) dataset is the most comprehensive pooled data available on cultural beliefs and values for more than 90 societies, it has data limitations with regard to generalizability of results to countries that are not included in the survey. To test generalizability I carried out a two independent t-test for levels of terrorism and other important socio-economic and political indicators for WVS countries and countries not included in the survey using Quality of Government (QOG) and GTD data for 194 countries for the year 1994 and 2000, for which data is available for all the variables. The results show that the WVS countries are overall not statistically representative of the rest of the countries (see Appendix 4-F). This could be a result of a selection bias of the countries selected for survey, due to accessibility or resource constraints. Another data limitation inherent in any survey data is the problem of measurement or response bias.

The results for incidents of terrorism as dependent variable are reported in Table-4.2 and the results of the second dependent variable i.e. the number of people killed, are presented in Table-4.3. The models do not assume causality but attempt to examine statistical relationship between religion and lethality in a controlled manner.

4.5 Interpretation

The results indicate that religiousness of a society impacts the lethality of an attack but has no significant impact on the number of terror incidents. Model-1 in Table-4.2 and Table-4.3 is the baseline model without any religion score. Table-4.2 (Model-2 and Model-3) shows that religiousness has no influence on the number of attacks a country experiences, and are not supportive of the first hypothesis which proposed that more religious societies suffer more terrorist incidents. This implies that both highly religious and less religious societies are vulnerable to terrorist attacks.

The estimation of religiousness on lethality of attack is presented in Table-4.2. The results show that more religiousness and higher religiosity score are associated with higher number of fatalities. As expected the coefficient for religiousness is negative which mean that more religious a society, the higher the number of people killed in an attack. The scale for religiousness is set up as 1 for high religiousness and 10 for low religiousness. So a one-unit increase in this variable actually means decrease in religious attitudes. We can interpret the result as a one point decrease in religiousness in a society leads to about 29 less people killed in terrorist attacks in a year. This confirms the second hypothesis that more religious societies are likely to experience more lethal terrorism.

For religiosity scale, which is a score of six questions from 0 to 100, as expected the coefficient is positive, meaning higher the religiosity score of a society, higher the lethality of terrorism experienced by the country. This result is also supportive of

Hypothesis-2. It is significant only at 10 percent level (see Table-4.3, Model-3) and shows that a one unit increase in religiosity of a society leads to about 2 more people killed in terrorist attacks in a year.

Table-4.3, Model-4, present the estimation of the third hypothesis i.e. societies, with higher percentage of Muslims experiences more fatal terrorist attacks. This model controls for religiousness in a country in a year to check for impact of percentage of Muslim population on lethality of terrorism. The results reject this hypothesis because the number of Muslim population appears to have no impact on lethality of an attack. This is an important finding as it debunks popular assumptions of associating Muslim populations with presence and operations of more lethal terrorist organizations. It confirms Juergensmeyer's argument that religious radicals from all major religious traditions have employed lethal terrorism and one religion cannot be associated with terrorism.

Overall most of the control variables are statistically insignificant at 5 percent level, except past incidents, which is positive and statistically significant. This means that if a country experienced terror attack last year, more people are killed in terror attack this year, indicating that terrorist organizations learn from past experience and improve methods to kill more people over time. Another variable that matters is population (see Table-4.3, Model-2). The relationship is statistically significant and positive which implies that countries with bigger populations suffer more lethal attacks. A larger population is usually a more heterogeneous one giving rise to conflicting interests and possibility of complex intersectional inequalities. Also bigger populations present an attractive target for terrorists and also it is harder for governments to monitor and control terrorist operations in bigger populations.

4.6 Conclusion

The results tell us about the statistical association of religiousness of a society and terrorism. Based on the available data on 76 countries for 1981-2004 we can predict that more religious societies suffer more lethal terrorist attacks. And this indicates that certain sections in religious societies provide community support to extremist ideologies, which lowers the operational costs of the terrorist groups to carry out a massively fatal attack. This study finds that more religious societies suffer more deadly attacks, and in the presence of previous evidence that religious terrorist organizations are more lethal (Asal & Rethemeyer, 2008b), the results posit a possible link between religious societies and religious organizations. Killing more people in religious societies becomes easier because religious extremists find sympathetic supporters in more religious societies than less religious ones. Terrorists with religious ideologies frequently employ theological texts or claims of divine inspiration to sanctify indiscriminate bloodshed in pursuit of their cause, and religious societies are more receptive to these interpretations. This resonates with the theoretical underpinnings of religious extremists using the concept of 'othering' to sanctify killing people of the out-group, and within religious societies the process of 'othering' is more deadly because religious terms are deployed to justify lethal tactics.

Terrorist organizations often rally public support by providing essential social services that states fail to provide to marginalized communities. This indicates a possible connection between religious societies and recruitment process for religious terrorist organizations. Suicide bombing is the most lethal means of terrorism and its essential requirement is human capital. The results imply that in more religious societies these organizations have higher probability of finding recruits who are convinced of their ideology and are ready to join the holy war between 'good' and 'evil', making suicide terrorism easier to accomplish. However this study recognizes that these links are not straightforward and linear since other socio-political and economic factors also play a significant and important role in the decision and design to carry out a lethal attack. Studies show that in the absence of state support and delivery of social services and welfare policies, certain extremist factions fill that gap and manipulate public support to perpetuate terrorism. They work with mutual aid arrangements and provide essential services to the marginalized populations, gaining support, sympathies and new recruits for violence. Research suggests that it is feelings of marginalization, deprivation and grievances that stimulate terrorism. In order to ameliorate terrorism, there is need to devise policies that address the root causes of despair, hopelessness and grievances.

The connection between providing social services and terrorism has important policy implications. States must take up the responsibility to ensure social justice and provision of essential social services to all its citizens regardless of their background and beliefs. Research shows that more equitable societies are more peaceful (Bjarnegård & Melander, 2011). Therefore building an equitable society based on norms of inclusion and social justice to bring marginalized communities into mainstream political, social and economic spheres is integral for sustainable peace and security. Social welfare policies and better governance minimizes the opportunity to build public support that extremist organizations exploit. These policies might not give immediate and dramatic results but they are critical for effective control of terrorism on a sustainable basis. Experience shows that military solutions may be appropriate in certain situations but they have limited effectiveness, as it creates more grievances and resentments and even new recruits. A broad based and multi-dimensional approach for improved political, social and economic conditions, especially for oppressed and marginalized communities, can help mitigate conditions that trigger grievances and propel religious terrorism. Henceforth a workable solution lies in building stronger democratic governments with effective social welfare systems that ensure the delivery of essential services to all its citizens regardless of religion, ethnicity, geography or political affiliation. It is important to devise long-term counter terrorism policies that include revisiting discriminatory budgetary priorities and use of development aid, political representation, support of local democracy, protection of minority rights, civil and human rights, gender and religious equality, provision of basic services and protection against negative effects of globalization.

Another important finding is that higher percentage of Muslim population is not significantly associated with lethality of an attack. This is a critical finding keeping in mind the current stereotypes regarding Muslim populations residing in various societies. It implies that religious fundamentalism is not restricted or limited to any one religion. This study provides a new insight into global terrorism and religiousness of societies belonging to any religious tradition.

This study recognizes that not all terrorist groups who profess religious ideology are acting according to their religious teachings, or that groups who claim secular ideologies are completely disengaged from political religion. While studying religion we have to proceed with caution not to equate religion with religiously motivated terrorism. As Juergensmeyer (2001) rightly points out that 'Osama bin Laden is no more representative of Islam than Timothy McVeigh is of Christianity, or Japan's Shoko Asahara is of Buddhism' (p1). This understanding calls for a collaborative multi-disciplinary approach since religion is tied to violence and terrorism in multiple and complex ways. Though religion is not violent per se and does not ordinarily lead to violence, however within a particular set of political, social and ideological circumstances it has the potential of extreme brutality (Juergensmeyer, 2000).

The theoretical understanding of the relationship between religion and terrorism needs more sophisticated analysis to unpack the key processes and structures of these connections that must be disrupted in order to curb terrorism. In fact the key to dissolve this relationship lies in religion itself, which is also the most powerful force to propagate peace and harmony. Religion possesses incredible power to mobilize people and given its strong institutional public role it has a unique power to build consensus, promote reconciliation and peace amongst conflicting parties. Counter terrorism policies in religious societies will be more effective if they appreciate the role or religion and policy makers are conscience of connections between religion and violence. Religion is a double-edged sword, and hope lies in propagating its peaceful message and practices. No society can be devoid of the potent force of religion, and it is exceedingly important to create space for social tolerance for religious diversity, freedom and equality for all religions and beliefs within a society.

This paper presents a statistical model that can be employed by policy makers to predict impact of terrorist attacks. This study is limited by data constraints and can only estimate for the self-reported religious attitudes and recorded terror attacks and resulting fatalities. The impact of terrorism reverberates beyond immediate reported damage, deaths and injuries, to psychological, cultural, sociological and political aspects of a society, which are not captured by the available terrorism data. This paper raises important gaps in terrorism data collection and collation. In addition the World Values Survey needs improvement in survey design for better coverage, and framing of survey questions to obtain more accurate responses and information. The 76 countries of this study are not representatives of rest of the countries, thus care should be taken to generalize these results to countries and period not covered in this study.

Future studies should explore sectarian violence within religious terrorism studies. All major world religions have a wide range of followers with a broad spectrum interpretations and understandings. More fine grain data collection and empirical analysis is vital for a better understanding of the complex relationship between religion and violence within these various sects and groups. The Global Terrorism Database used in this study is at a country year level, so it was not possible to test for the kind of attack. More research is needed to find the causal mechanisms between suicide bombing and religious attitudes of a society. Better terrorism data is needed to differentiate between perpetrator and target countries to understand state factors that produce terrorism, and the factors that render countries to be juicer targets. Another important way to examine this question would be to look at how religiousness affects the number of terrorist organizations active in different societies, for which we need cross sectional time series organizational based data, which is currently unavailable. Nevertheless further scholarship can consider examining this question as newer datasets become available.

Printed in the USA
CPSIA information can be obtained
at www.ICGtesting.com
LVHW020222130124
768887LV00075B/1931